Palm Reading Made Easy

You don't have to be psychic—you don't have to burn incense and candles—you don't have to wear a turban or scarves and tons of jewelry—to be a top-notch palm reader. This ancient method of reading character and destiny is practiced every day by thousands of ordinary people like you.

Until now, though, learning it hasn't been very easy. The first book on Western palmistry was written by Aristotle for Alexander the Great, and a lot of today's books on the subject read like they were written back then, too!

That's why best-selling author Richard Webster has written *Palm Reading for Beginners*. Here, in plain English, is a complete, fully illustrated guide to reading the story written in anyone's palm. From the basic meanings of the lines to the fine points of markings and complexion, these clear descriptions will have you revealing secrets and foretelling the future from the first day.

Whether your interest is casual or serious, be prepared for a rich, rewarding experience when you reach across to someone and say, "Show me your palm."

About the Author

Richard Webster was born in Auckland, New Zealand in 1946. New Zealand is still his home, though he travels widely every year lecturing and conducting workshops on psychic subjects around the world. He is a prolific author and also writes monthly columns for two magazines. Richard began his working life in publishing, and became in turn a bookstore proprietor, pianist, stage hypnotist, palmist, ghostwriter, and magician before becoming a professional teacher and writer on psychic topics.

To Write to the Author

If you wish to contact the author or would like more information about this book, you may write to the author in care of Llewellyn Worldwide, and we will forward your request. Both the author and the publisher appreciate hearing from you and learning of your enjoyment of this book and how it has helped you. Llewellyn Worldwide cannot guarantee that every letter written to the author can be answered, but all will be forwarded. Please write to:

Richard Webster
℅ Llewellyn Worldwide Ltd.
P.O. Box 64383, Dept. K791-9
St. Paul, MN 55164-0383, U.S.A.

Please enclose a self-addressed, stamped envelope for reply,
or $1.00 to cover costs. If outside U.S.A., enclose international
postal reply coupon.

Palm Reading
for BEGINNERS

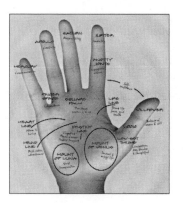

Find Your

Future in

the Palm

of Your

Hand

Richard Webster

2000
Llewellyn Publications
St. Paul, Minnesota, 55164-0383, U.S.A.

FIRST EDITION
Second Printing, 2000

Cover design by Lisa Novak
Interior illustrations by Jeannie Ferguson
Editing and interior design by Eila Savela

Library of Congress Cataloging-in-Publication Data
Webster, Richard, 1946–
    Palm reading for beginners : find your future in the palm of your
    hand / Richard Webster.--1st. ed.
        p. cm.
    Includes bibliographical references (p.) and index.
    ISBN: 1–56718–791–9
    1. Palmistry   I. Title.

BF921 .W4 2000
133.6--dc21   00-025070
                                                              CIP

Llewellyn Worldwide does not participate in, endorse, or have any authority or
responsibility concerning private business transactions between our authors and
the public.
    All mail addressed to the author is forwarded but the publisher cannot, unless
specifically instructed by the author, give out an address or phone number.

Llewellyn Publications
A Division of Llewellyn Worldwide, Ltd.
P.O. Box 64383, Dept. K791–9
St. Paul, Minnesota 55164-0383, U.S.A.
www.llewellyn.com

Printed in the United States of America

Dedication

For my good friend Carl Herron,
gifted psychic, humorist, philosopher,
and publisher of *The Path*

Other Books by Richard Webster

Astral Travel for Beginners
Aura Reading for Beginners
Chinese Numerology
Dowsing for Beginners
Feng Shui for Apartment Living
Feng Shui for Beginners
Feng Shui for Love and Romance
Feng Shui for Success and Happiness
Feng Shui for the Workplace
Feng Shui in the Garden
Numerology Magic
Omens, Oghams, and Oracles
101 Feng Shui Tips for the Home
Revealing Hands
Seven Secrets to Success
Spirit Guides and Angel Guardians

Table of Contents

Illustrations

Introduction

Palmistry is one of the oldest of the occult arts. People have been fascinated with hands since time began. There are imprints of palms in the innermost parts of the Santander Caves in Spain, showing how important hands were to people in Stone Age times.

The most important moment in human evolution occurred when man began to stand upright. This meant that the hands, which up until then had been used as front feet, were now able to be used for other purposes. In fact, they became an extension of the human mind. More room is taken up in the brain for the different activities of our hands than for any other organ of the body. It is fascinating to watch newborn babies interact with the world using their hands. Even something as simple as touch has to be learned.

The brain sends messages to the hands, instructing them to perform any number of intricate tasks. Many of these tasks have had to be learned in the first place, but become automatic as soon as they are mastered. Writing with a pen is a good example of this. The hands also send information to the brain. If you have ever touched something hot, you know exactly how quickly that information is sent to the brain.

At some stage people realized that every hand is different, and from this discovery palmistry began. The fact that no two hands are the same must have intrigued primitive people. One explanation for this can be found in the Bible: "He sealeth up the hand of every man, that all men may know His work" (Job 37:7).[1]

Primitive man was also able to make practical use of this information. Thumbprints and fingerprints were used instead of signatures. In China there are numerous examples of important papers that have been "signed" with the thumbprint of the emperor.

Some 2,600 years ago Aristotle wrote a book on palmistry for Alexander the Great, and there is nothing in that book that a modern-day palmist would dispute. Consequently, the basic principles of palmistry have been around for a long time.

Palmistry has had an extremely varied history. At times it has been revered, while at other periods it was considered the work of the devil. Unfortunately, different superstitions were added to palmistry over the years, and these caused many people to discredit the subject without evaluating it further.

Palmistry was first treated in a scientific manner in France during the nineteenth century. A man called Adolphe Desbarrolles investigated palmistry with the intention of disproving it. However, his research convinced him of the validity of the subject, and eventually he wrote a monumental book on palmistry.[2]

At about the same time, a retired army officer called Stanislas d'Arpentigny discovered a remarkable fact. He had become friendly with a couple who entertained on a regular basis. D'Arpentigny found that most of the guests at the parties arranged by the husband had short, blunt hands with stubby fingers. The guests invited to the wife's soirees had hands that were shapely, slender, and had long fingers.

D'Arpentigny began studying palmistry and developed a system of hand classification that is still used by many palmists today. He also wrote a book on the subject.[3]

In 1900 William Benham, an American, published his monumental book *The Laws of Scientific Handreading*. In this book he explained how to read palms scientifically. Up until then, most people believed that you had to be psychic in order to read palms.

Since then, a number of people have followed in his footsteps. Psychologists became interested in how accurate palmistry is in revealing character, and many books have been written from a psychological point of view. The first of these was published in 1848 by Dr. Carl Gustav Carus, who was the personal physician to the king of Saxony. His book (*Die Symbolik der Menschlichen Gestalt und Ueber Grund und Bedeutung der Verschiedenen Formen der Hand*) related the fingers of the hand to the person's conscious mind, and the palm to the subconscious.

Since the end of World War II, the Kennedy-Galton Center, attached to the University of London, has been studying palms scientifically, using them to determine the predisposition of people towards certain illnesses. Certainly, nothing could be more important than health, and it is

exciting that modern-day scientists are proving scientifically what palmists have known for thousands of years.

By taking up palmistry you will be joining a tradition
that has lasted for thousands of years.

I first became interested in the subject as a young boy. I
used to regularly visit a neighbor who was an excellent
cook. I was a keen reader and was fascinated to discover
that she and her husband had a large library in their home.
I would sit in their library for hours, eating her scones and
cakes, and looking at the books on every wall.

One day I noticed a large section of books on palmistry.
These belonged to her husband, who was a palmist. Palmistry was illegal in New Zealand at the time, and he used to
give readings quietly and secretly. I think it amused him to
find a small child showing interest in this subject, and he
taught me some of the basics of palmistry. I would go to
school and look at the palms of the other students, but did
not take the subject seriously until I reached puberty and
discovered what a wonderful way it was to meet girls!

Since then I have read thousands and thousands of
palms. I have made my living in several different countries
with this skill. For some years I used to do quick palm readings in shopping malls and would see hundreds of palms
every week. At one time I conducted horoscope parties,
which were mind reading demonstrations in people's
homes. The most exciting part of these evenings, from the
guests' point of view, was the private palm reading they
received after the demonstration.

Palmistry has been very good to me, and I am grateful to it for the many opportunities it has given me over the years. I am still as enthusiastic about palmistry as I was as a teenager, and hope that you will pick up some of this enthusiasm as you read this book.

1

The Whole Hand

You do not necessarily need to examine the lines on the palm to read a hand. You can tell a great deal about a person simply from the shape, resilience, color, and texture of his or her hand.

Major and Minor Hands

We each have two hands, which are described as the major and minor hands in palmistry. The major hand is the one you use most naturally. If you are right-handed, it will be your right hand. Naturally, it will be your left hand if you are left-handed.

Traditionally, the major hand was the one that records what you do with your life, while the minor hand reveals the skills, talents, and qualities you were born with. However, although there is some truth in this, it does not give the whole story.

Our hands change as we progress through life. Even our minor hands change, and this would not be the case if they simply showed what we were born with. Consequently, I consider the major hand to reveal what the person is actually doing, while the minor hand shows what the person is thinking about. It is still a map of potentials, but it changes to reflect what the person wants to do. Naturally, this can be completely different to what the person is doing in his or her everyday life.

Consequently, you need to examine both hands when giving a palm reading. When I am doing quick readings, perhaps in a party situation, I will look at the major hand only. However, I always study both hands when giving a serious reading.

Skin Texture

It is easier to determine the person's skin texture by looking at the back of the hand. The skin texture is the quality of the skin, and this can range all the way from fine and smooth, to rough and coarse.

The skin texture reveals how refined the person is. Someone with an extremely fine skin texture that is silky and smooth like a baby will be sensitive, gentle, and refined in outlook. This person will be easily disturbed by anything that affects his or her sensitivities.

Conversely, someone with coarse skin will be rougher, more down-to-earth, and less high-strung than someone with a fine skin texture. This person will be straightforward and direct.

The skin texture gives you an immediate clue about how the person functions in life. For instance, it would be hard to imagine someone with coarse hands selling beautiful works of art. However, this person might do extremely well selling engineering supplies.

Consistency

We can pick up a great deal of information by shaking someone's hand. Someone who takes your hand with a firm grip conveys a better immediate impression than someone who offers a clammy, lifeless hand.

After you have determined the skin texture from the back of the hand, turn the person's hands over and gently press on the palms.

Consistency is determined by the degree of elasticity in the hand. Hand consistency varies from extremely hard to soft and spongy.

People with hands that are soft and spongy are sensual pleasure seekers who do the least amount of work they can get away with. They function best in comfortable surroundings, where they can daydream and laze their lives away.

People with firmer, more resilient hands are practical, energetic, and hard-working. They enjoy challenges and need to keep busy in order to be happy.

Flexibility

The flexibility of the person's mind is determined by the flexibility of his or her palm. People with flexible hands are adaptable and can quickly adjust to changing circumstances. People with rigid hands are inflexible, stubborn, and rigid.

To determine the flexibility of someone's hand I rest the back of his or her hand on my fingers while pressing against his or her fingertips with my thumb. Some people have hands that feel like a block of wood, while others have hands that bend back and almost create a right angle. Most people's hands fall somewhere between these two extremes.

Color

The color of the hand provides valuable clues about the person's health and temperament. Naturally, the colors of our hands change depending on the temperature. The chances are that people are simply feeling cold if their hands appear blue. They may have just come inside after being out in the snow. However, there is a palmistry interpretation if the room temperature is normal, but the person's hands have a bluish tinge.

People with white hands, for instance, are likely to be anemic. This results in a lack of vitality and energy. These people are unfeeling and selfish. They become irritable and upset easily. They are self-sufficient, idealistic, and cold.

Hands with a yellowish tinge to them belong to people who have a slightly jaundiced view of the world. Bluish hands show that the person's blood circulation is poor.

Pinkish hands are considered normal in people with a European descent. This is a good sign and show that the person is loving, appreciative, sympathetic, and supportive.

Red hands belong to people with a great deal of energy. It is important that this energy is used wisely. People with red hands can lose their temper very easily. Sometimes, the redness is visible on only part of the hand. When this occurs, the energies of that particular part of the palm are increased.

The Shape of the Hand

There are a number of different ways of classifying the hand, but by far the simplest is to see if the palm itself is square or oblong in shape.

Square Palm

People with a square-shaped palm are down-to-earth, capable, practical people. They enjoy a challenge and are prepared to work long and hard, when required, to achieve their goals. They have plenty of stamina and energy.

Oblong Palm

Oblong palms are the hands that artists love. These hands are long and shapely, but are much less practical than square hands. People with oblong palms enjoy coming up with ideas, but these often remain daydreams and are seldom put into action. These people are creative, idealistic, and gentle.

This divides the entire human race into just two categories. We can double this by examining the fingers, and classifying them as short or long. Usually, it is a simple matter to determine if the fingers are short or long in proportion to the palm. However, at times it can be difficult to decide. If this is the case, ask the person to fold their fingers over the palm. If the fingers reach more than seven-eighths of the way down the palm they are said to be long. Even this is not perfect, though, since some people have more flexible hands and fingers than others. If it is impossible to determine if the fingers are long or short in proportion to the palm, they are obviously medium in length.

Short Fingers

People with short fingers are quick on the uptake, and become impatient with people who take all day. They like to get in, do the job, and get out again as quickly as possible. They enjoy being busy, and frequently tackle a number of different tasks, all at the same time. They are often better at starting than they are at finishing. They prefer the broad, overall view and do not enjoy the details.

Long Fingers

People with long fingers enjoy work that is detailed and involved. They are patient and like to take whatever time is needed to finish a task properly. They enjoy finishing what they start. They are conscientious, responsible, and like to get down to the bottom of things to understand what makes them work.

Medium Fingers

Many people have fingers that are neither long nor short. These people are a mixture of the qualities of people who have short and long fingers.

Consequently, they can be patient at times, but impatient at others. They are conscientious and responsible most of the time, but can do a slapdash job if the task does not appeal to them very much.

Knowledge of finger length alone can be useful to you in your daily life. If you have to wait in line somewhere, try to choose a line that is waiting for a cashier with short fingers. That person's line will move more quickly than that of a long-fingered cashier who will want to double-check everything. The short-fingered cashier will try to deal with people as quickly as possible and will worry about balancing the cash register at the end of the day.

However, there will also be occasions when you will want the person you are dealing with to pay particular attention to the details. In this case, select someone with the longest fingers you can find.

Hand Classification

We now have four possible combinations: a square hand with short fingers, a square hand with long fingers, an oblong hand with short fingers, and an oblong hand with long fingers. These four types can be related to the four elements: earth, air, fire, and water.

Earth Hand

An earth hand is a square hand with short fingers (figure 1). Earth hands usually have few lines on them, though the lines that are present are well marked. These people are always busy and enjoy doing things with their hands. They are practical, careful, reliable, and solid. However, they can also be impatient, suspicious, critical, and easily roused. They enjoy the outdoors and prefer quiet lifestyles, away from the hustle and bustle of large cities. They enjoy the feel of soil, and like working with the earth in some sort of way. They are usually free of stress and take life exactly as it comes. This philosophy means that they usually enjoy good health and lead long, fruitful lives.

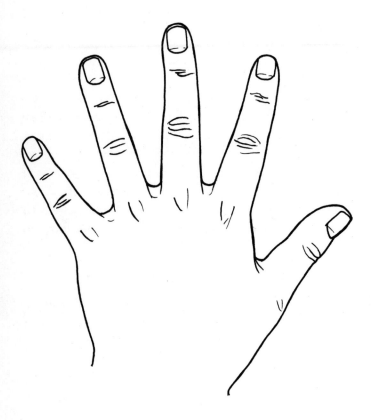

Figure 1: Earth Hand

Air Hand

An air hand consists of a square palm and long fingers (figure 2). These people are inventive, innovative, practical, and thoughtful. They are conscientious, good with details, and need constant challenges. The air hand belongs to someone who is more intellectual than someone with an earth hand. Despite this emphasis on the intellect, people with air hands also possess a strong intuition. They can make their minds up rapidly, using a combination of logic and feeling. They enjoy expressing themselves and are easy to get along with. They have an inquisitive nature that keeps them perpetually young. They are refined and express themselves well. They are interested in travel, communication, freedom, and anything that is slightly out of the ordinary.

Fire Hand

A fire hand consists of an oblong palm and short fingers (figure 3). These people are imaginative, enthusiastic, versatile, and impatient. They have great ideas, but need to evaluate them carefully to make sure that they are practical before starting on them. They are better at the broad brush strokes than the fine details, and often lose interest before the task is completed. Their changeable natures can sometimes be frustrating to others, but usually they are able to carry people along with their energy and excitement. They are generous, sociable, and gregarious. Fire people need to be busy to be happy. They would not last long in any occupation that was too simple, dull, or boring.

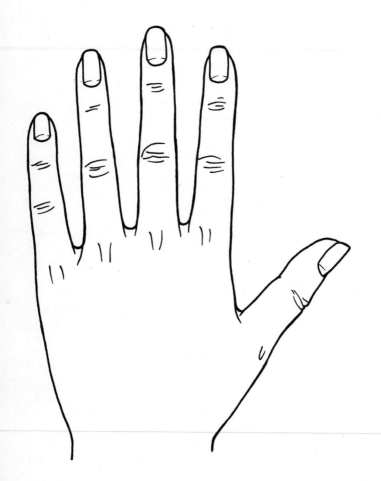

Figure 2: Air Hand

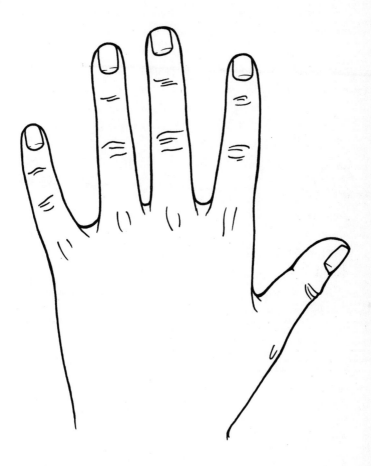

Figure 3: Fire Hand

Water Hand

A water hand consists of an oblong palm and long fingers (figure 4). This is the shape that is loved by artists, but is not overly practical in daily life. People with water hands lead rich emotional lives, and are extremely imaginative and sensitive. Consequently, they do well in any career that involves creativity and a strong aesthetic sense. They are basically idealistic and feel constantly let down by the actions of people with hands shaped differently than theirs. They are receptive, changeable, and impressionable. They are also sympathetic and have a great love for all living things. They give the impression of being calm and in control, but inwardly suffer from nervous tension and worry.

This system of hand classification is the one that is most useful nowadays, since everyone can be classified into one of the four groups. However, the system that d'Arpentigny developed last century that classified people into seven groups is still being used, and you will find it useful to know something about it. This was the system that I was taught originally, and I still occasionally mentally classify people into one of these categories. However, the four element classification system is the one that I use most of the time.

Elementary Hand

The elementary hand is somewhat clumsy in appearance (figure 5). The palm is square in shape and the fingers are short, stubby, and relatively shapeless. The skin is coarse and the back of the hand is frequently hairy. The palm contains few lines, sometimes as few as two or three. These people are

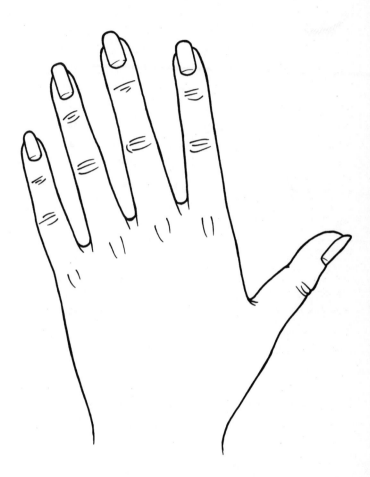

Figure 4: Water Hand

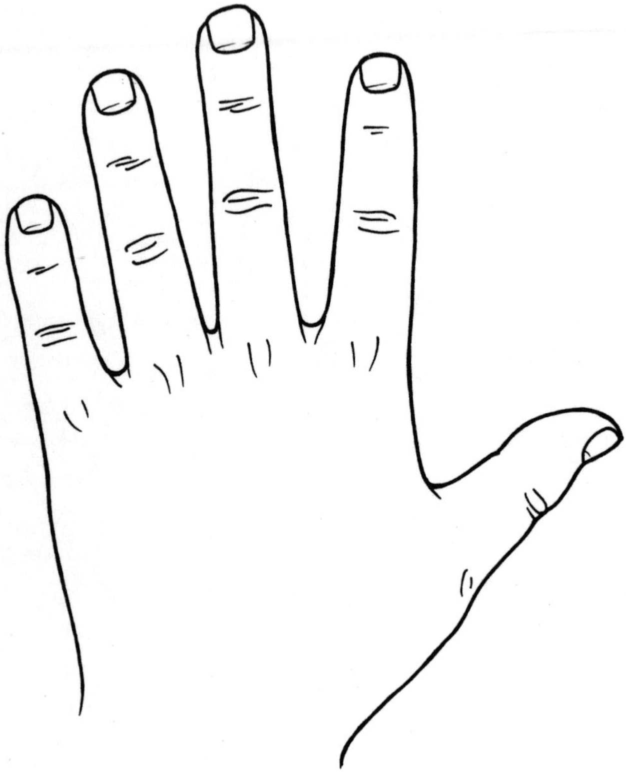

Figure 5: Elementary Hand

stubborn and find it hard to express themselves in words. They take life pretty much as comes, living for today, and making few plans for the future. These people are good with their hands, and can sometimes be extremely creative.

This hand was found frequently at the time that d'Arpentigny developed his system. He found many peasant farmers with elementary hands. However, this type of hand has become increasingly uncommon, and, in practice, you will only occasionally find a true elementary hand.

Practical Hand

The practical hand also has a square-shaped palm, but the fingers are longer, and better shaped than those belonging to the elementary hand (figure 6). D'Arpentigny called the practical hand "square or useful." The skin is not as coarse on the practical hand as it is on the earth hand, and there are more lines on the palm. People with practical hands can turn their hands to anything, which is why this shape is called "practical." They respect authority and are conservative in outlook. They are disciplined, predictable conformists who keep their feet firmly on the ground. They are cautious, reliable, and orderly.

Spatulate Hand

This hand is similar to the practical hand, but the fingertips resemble a spatula and flare at the ends (figure 7). D'Arpentigny called these "spatulate or active" hands. People with spatulate hands are energetic, persistent, and independent. They are prepared to work hard, just as long as their efforts are rewarded. They overindulge at times, and generally prefer quantity to quality in all things.

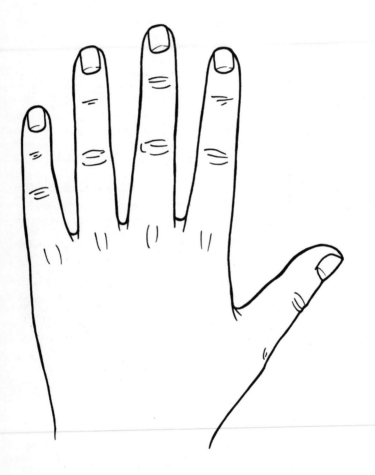

Figure 6: Practical Hand

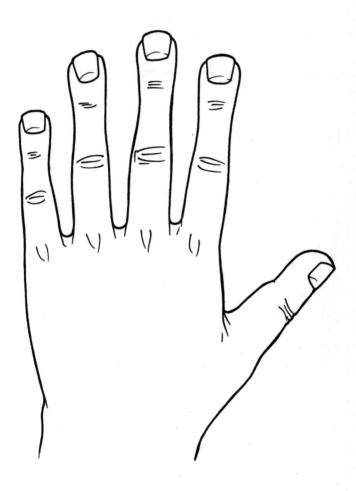

Figure 7: Spatulate Hand

Conic Hand

The conic hand is graceful, curved, and attractive in appearance (figure 8). The palm is slightly oblong, and the fingers are long with rounded tips. The palm is inclined to feel fleshy. People with conic hands are creative, aesthetic, and desire a perfect world. They dislike coarseness of any sort. They have a desire to succeed, but generally prefer to daydream about success rather than undertake the hard work that is necessary for any achievement.

Psychic Hand

The psychic hand is long, slender, and graceful (figure 9). It is extremely attractive, but is essentially impractical, since these people spend much of their time in a fantasy world, escaping the realities of life. These people are idealistic and highly intuitive. They are also sensitive, loving, and easily hurt. The psychic hand is an extreme form of the water hand.

Philosophical Hand

The philosophical hand is squarish in shape, and has long fingers with obvious joints (figure 10). Because of this, philosophical hands are often called "knotty hands." These people like to analyze everything carefully before acting. In my classes I used to tell my students to imagine thoughts coming in through the tips of the fingers, reaching the first joint and going round and around before moving on to the second joint where the process is repeated. Consequently, by the time the thought reaches the palm it has been thoroughly analyzed. This is why people with philosophical hands want to know the reasons behind everything and prefer to

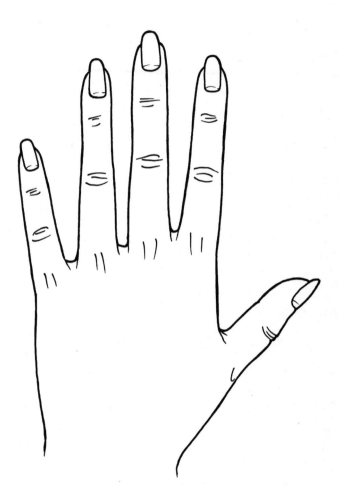

Figure 8: Conic Hand

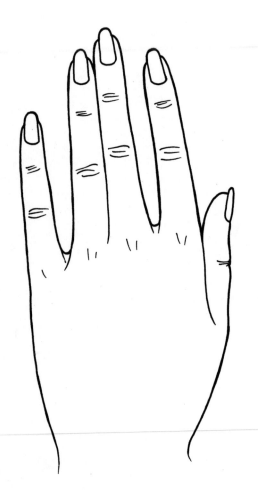

Figure 9: Psychic Hand

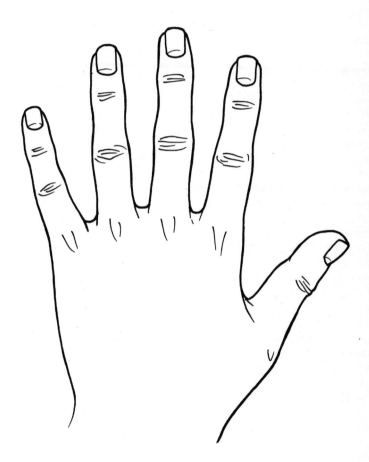

Figure 10: Philosophical Hand

find things out for themselves. People with philosophical hands go their own way and do not care what other people think about them. Consequently, they are usually unorthodox and often eccentric.

Mixed Hand

The problem with d'Arpentigny's system is that not everyone slots neatly into any of his classifications. Consequently, he had a mixed hand, which was used for anyone who had hands that were not elementary, practical, conic, psychic, or philosophical (figure 11).

Many hands are a mixture of two, three, or even four of d'Arpentigny's types. The palm might be practical, but have psychic fingers with prominent (philosophical) joints.

In practice, the only true types you are likely to find using d'Arpentigny's system of classification are people with conic or philosophical hands.

There are many other systems of hand classification. Desbarrolles, for instance, divided hands into three groups, based largely on the shapes of the fingertips. No one system is perfect. As you have just seen, d'Arpentigny had to introduce a "mixed" hand to classify every shape that did not fit neatly into the other types. In the 1950s, George Muchary devised a system that divided people into eight groups.[1] It is interesting to experiment with the different systems, but the first one that we discussed (earth, air, fire, and water) is the one that I have found most useful and easiest to use.

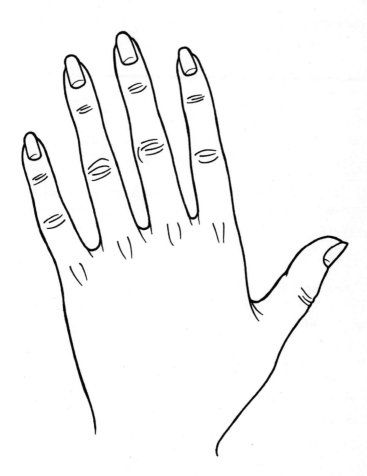

Figure 11: Mixed Hand

The Four Quadrants

The hand can be divided into four sections by two imaginary lines (figure 12). The first runs down the middle of the second finger and continues on to the wrist. This divides the hand into two halves. The half that contains the thumb is the outer-directed part of the hand and relates to what we do in the world. The other half is inner-directed and relates to our thoughts.

The second imaginary line begins under the thumb, halfway between the base of the fingers and the wrist. It is a horizontal line that runs across the palm, bisecting the first imaginary line. The half of the hand that includes the fingers relates to activity, while the other half is more receptive and passive.

These two lines create four quadrants: the active-outer, active-inner, passive-outer, and passive-inner. Often, when you look at a palm, you will notice that one of these four quadrants is more prominent than the others. This may simply be a feeling, while at other times, it is obviously more developed than the other quadrants. If all the quadrants appear to be equal, the person has managed to effectively balance the different areas of his or her life.

Active-Outer Quadrant

The active-outer quadrant includes the top part of the thumb, and the first finger and half of the second finger. This area relates to the person's goals and aspirations. If this quadrant is prominent, the person will put a great deal of thought and hard work into achieving his or her goals. He or she will be enthusiastic, energetic, persistent, and impatient.

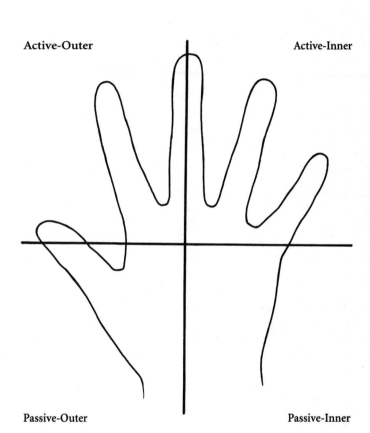

Figure 12: The Four Quadrants

Passive-Outer Quadrant

The passive-outer quadrant includes the bottom part of the thumb and the mound immediately below it (mount of Venus). This quadrant is concerned with physical stamina and sexuality. When this area is well developed the person will have a great deal of energy and stamina, as well as a strong sexual appetite. Conversely, if this area is less developed than the other quadrants, the person will have little interest in physical activities, and will generally lack enthusiasm and energy.

Active-Inner Quadrant

The active-inner quadrant includes the ring and little fingers, plus half of the second finger. When this quadrant is emphasized, the person will be interested in learning and the arts, and will have little interest in worldly success.

Passive-Inner Quadrant

The passive-inner quadrant occupies the area known as the mount of Luna, and is the quarter of the palm that is directly opposite the thumb. This area is related to the creative subconscious. When this area is well developed the person will be imaginative, intuitive, sensitive, and empathetic. He or she is likely to be involved in some form of creativity.

Fleshy Palms

When you start looking at people's hands you will quickly notice that some appear to be fleshier or much more padded than others. In some cases the palm will feel almost spongy to the touch. People with fleshy, well-padded palms enjoy the luxuries of life, and will overindulge on occasion. People with palms that feel hard to the touch are less interested in indulging themselves in this way, and can stay away from different pleasures if other things seem more important at the time. People with palms that are firm to the touch can better withstand the ups and downs of life than people with fleshy palms.

Coarse and Refined Hands

Calluses caused by hard physical work do not create coarse hands. Coarse hands are ones that have highly obvious pores in the skin. These are often more visible on the back of the hand than they are on the palm. People with coarse hands have animal instincts and are perfectly happy as long as their basic needs are being met. They are also extremely "thick-skinned."

People with refined hands are more cultured and aesthetic. They appreciate nice things, and want their home and work environments to be as pleasant and as attractive as possible.

Hair

A small amount of hair is desirable on the back of a man's hand and denotes masculinity. A large amount of hair reveals someone with strong physical appetites that have to be met for the person to be happy.

Size

The size of the hands denotes what the person wants to do with them. Strangely enough, people with large hands enjoy working with small, intricate, detailed things. The largest hands I have ever seen belonged to a man who enjoyed a worldwide reputation as a watchmaker. People with small hands like to do things on a big scale and want to undertake big projects.

How the Hand Is Held

Interestingly, you can tell a great deal just from the way in which someone offers his or her hands to you. If the hand is shown with all the fingers touching, the person will be wary, cautious, and probably lacking in confidence. If the hand is displayed with the fingers widely spread, the person is likely to be outgoing, enthusiastic, and have nothing to hide. This person will be much more confident and self-assured than someone who holds their hands out with the fingers touching.

Often, people will show their hands to you with the fingers well spread, but as you start reading their palms, the fingers will gradually close. This shows that they are concerned that you will learn too much about them by looking at their palms.

Most people think that palmistry is concerned solely with the lines on the hand. As you can see, this is not the case, and you can tell a great deal from the size and shape of the hands. In the next chapter we will start looking at the lines on the palm.

2

The Major Lines

There are four major lines on the hand: the heart, head, life, and destiny lines. Together, they give a vivid picture of the quality of the person's life.

The heart line gives a clear picture of the person's emotional and love life. It reveals emotional energy.

The head line reveals how the person thinks. It reveals mental energy.

The life line shows how much the person enjoys life and how passionate he or she is about life. It reveals physical energy.

The destiny line gives a sense of purpose to the person's life. It shows that he or she has something to live for, and provides the necessary motivation and direction to become successful.

The interplay of these four lines shows exactly how the person is using his or her emotional, mental, and physical senses. Ideally, all four lines should be clear, well marked, and deep. Unfortunately, this is the exception, rather than the rule.

Many years ago, in India, I saw the palms of a man who had been unconscious for more than a year. All of the lines had disappeared, and the hand looked strangely empty. In practice, every now and again, you will find people with only three lines on their hands (heart, head, and life lines). People with only two lines will have the heart and head lines interconnected. This is known as a simian crease, and we will discuss that later.

Speaking generally, the fewer lines the person has on his or her hand, the easier that person's life will be. This is because most lines are caused by nervous tension and worry. However, someone with just two or three lines on his or her palms will lead a dull and uneventful life. In palmistry we are always looking for a balance. Three lines are far too few, and hundreds of fine lines of nervous energy are far too many.

I find it best to look at the lines in a specific order. I start with the heart line, followed by the head line, life line, and destiny line. This is because the heart line gives me information about the person's emotional life. After determining that, I turn to the head line which tells me about the person's intellect. After this, I look at the life line, which is actually the most important line on the hand. It tells me about the person's stamina and energy. Finally the destiny line tells me about their path through life. I gradually build up a picture of the whole person as I make my way along these lines.

Heart Line

The heart line is the major line that runs across the palm closest to the fingers. It starts at the side of the palm below the little finger, proceeds across the hand, and finishes in the area of the first or second fingers.

The heart line can either curve or remain reasonably straight at the end. A heart line that curves at the end is known as a physical heart line (figure 13). This line will end either close to the base of the first two fingers, or most commonly, somewhere in between them.

People with a physical heart line find it comparatively easy to express their innermost needs and feelings. They express themselves in a confident and assertive manner. When things go wrong, they pick themselves up quickly and carry on with their lives.

The other type of heart line is called a mental heart line. This runs straight across the palm and does not curve toward the fingers at the end (figure 14). People with this type of heart line find it harder to express their innermost feelings, and need to be told frequently that they are loved and desired. They are sensitive and easily hurt. They are inclined to bottle up their feelings and will suffer in silence rather than make a scene.

In a sense, the physical heart line is proactive, while the mental heart line is reactive.

Many years ago someone told me that people with mental heart lines need soft music, candlelight, and wine, while the back seat of an old car is all that's required by people with a physical heart line. This is an exaggeration, of course, but it gives some idea of the difference between these two

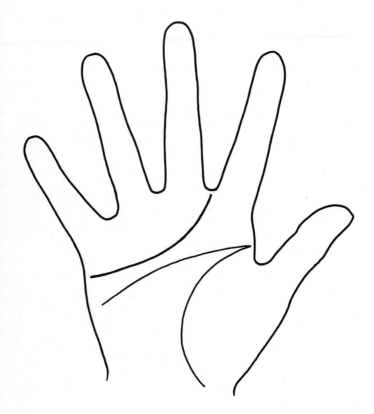

Figure 13: Physical Heart Line

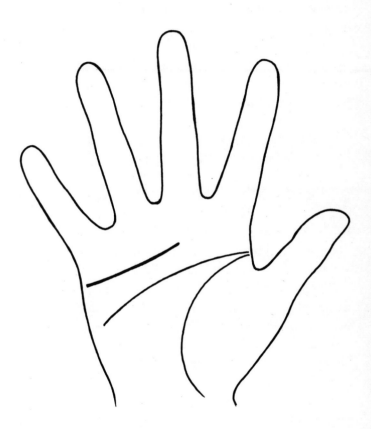

Figure 14: Mental Heart Line

types of heart line. Obviously, from a compatibility point of view, it is easier if the two partners have similar heart lines that end in the same place.

The heart line is related to the person's heart, and has a bearing on the person's physical well-being. Obviously, emotional ups and downs can affect the person's physical body. The heart line is also closely related to the soul, since the ability to love and be loved is connected to the divine.

The ending position of this line is important. If the heart line ends below the first finger (figure 15), the person is overly idealistic, and is likely to feel let down and disappointed at times by the actions of others. When the heart line ends under the second finger (figure 16), the person will be concerned only with his or her own needs, and will not have much interest in the needs of others. This person will have a lack of emotional involvement.

The easiest position for the heart line to end in is between the first and second fingers (figure 17). This gives a balance between extreme idealism and selfishness. This person will be concerned with both his or her own needs, but will also be interested in the needs of others. He or she will also be realistic and keep both feet firmly on the ground.

Some people have a heart line that splits in two near the end. This means that the person has some of the qualities of both the physical and mental heart lines. Consequently, he or she will have a complex emotional nature. People with a fork at the end of the heart line are able to see opposing points of view.

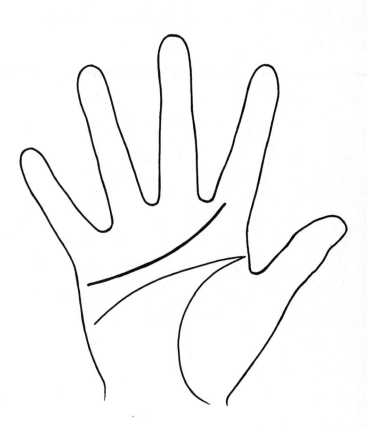

Figure 15: Heart Line Ending Below First Finger

Figure 16: Heart Line Ending Below Second Finger

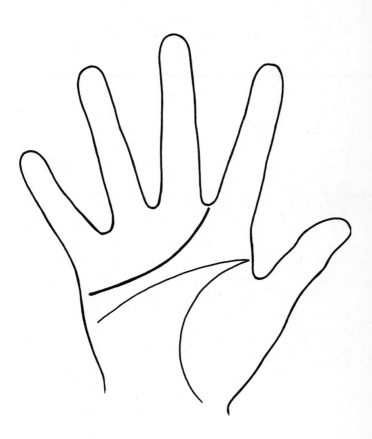

**Figure 17: Heart Line Ending Between First
and Second Fingers**

Occasionally, you will find a heart line that has split into three lines at the end. This is known as a "trident." It has no specific meaning, but generally denotes a fortunate life. However, I have noticed that this is only the case when the person is inside a strong, close, and stable relationship.

The heart line should be smooth and well marked for its entire length. Unfortunately, this is extremely uncommon. The heart line reflects our emotional lives, and we all have ups and downs at times. These are revealed on the heart line as "islands," or small ovals that look like braiding. They are sometimes referred to as "chains." They indicate the times of emotional tension in the person's life, when nothing was going smoothly. These are usually relationship problems. Consequently, it is easy to see if someone had a bad relationship followed by a good one. The heart line will be full of islands at the time of the difficult relationship, but will then become clear once the person has entered into the happy relationship.

A single island on the heart line is a sign of depression at the time indicated. Crosses and breaks on the line indicate a time of emotional loss. This usually marks the end of a relationship, which could mean a separation, or the death of the partner.

A heart line that is strong, well marked, deep, and reasonably clear shows that the person will be basically happy, and will enjoy a fruitful and stable emotional life.

Frequently, you will find a short fine line that runs parallel to the heart line at the very end. This is an extremely fortunate sign, showing that the person will enjoy a strong, long-lasting relationship that is still there in his or her old age. As many people are concerned about being lonely in their old age, I always point this out whenever I see it in a palm.

Head Line

The head line reveals the intellect and how the person uses his or her brain.

It starts on the side of the hand, between the base of the thumb and the first finger, and crosses the palm towards the little finger side. It either goes across in a reasonably straight line, or alternatively curves towards the wrist.

Again, this line should be clear and well marked. Any breaks or islands on this line indicate periods when the person's brain was not being utilized properly. A faint head line shows that the person has mental ability that is not being used.

This line can be long or short. The longer the line is, the more involved and detailed the person's thinking processes will be. People with short head lines are shrewd and think quickly. However, they skim over the surface and are not as interested in the details as people with long head lines. At one time it was believed that the longer the head line was, the more intelligent the person would be. This is certainly not the case, since the presence of a long head line is no guarantee that the person will use this ability. In fact, we all have an unlimited capacity to learn, and people with short head lines are certainly not disadvantaged in any way.

If the head line crosses the palm in a reasonably straight line and does not curve towards the wrist, the person is logical, practical, down-to-earth, and unimaginative (figure 18).

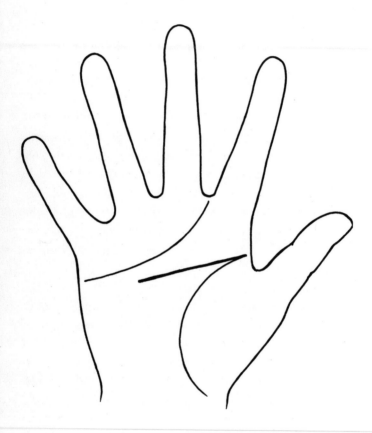

Figure 18: Unimaginative Head Line

When the head line curves towards the wrist, inside the area known as the passive-inner quadrant, the person will be imaginative and creative (figure 19). The greater the curve is, the more imaginative the person will be. This can come out in a variety of ways. It may simply indicate someone who tells lies, even when it is not necessary. It could indicate a poet, an actor, a musician, or even a daydreamer. We have to look at other aspects of the hand to determine how, and if, this creative potential is being used.

Many people have a fork on the end of the head line. This is known as the "writer's fork" and shows that the person can come up with good ideas and make them practical (figure 20). Writers do this, of course, but so do many other people. It gives an inventive slant to the brain, and has been a saving grace to many people with imaginative head lines. Not only do they come up with wonderful ideas, but they then get busy and make them happen.

If the head line has a distinct bend at the very end, the person will have strong material needs and will do whatever is required to satisfy those desires (figure 21).

The starting position is also important. If the head line touches the life line at the start, it denotes a cautious person who will think before acting (figure 22). When there is a gap between the start of the head line and the life line, the person will be independent and impulsive (figure 23). The larger the gap between these two lines, the more outspoken, impulsive, and independent the person will be.

Figure 19: Imaginative, Creative Head Line

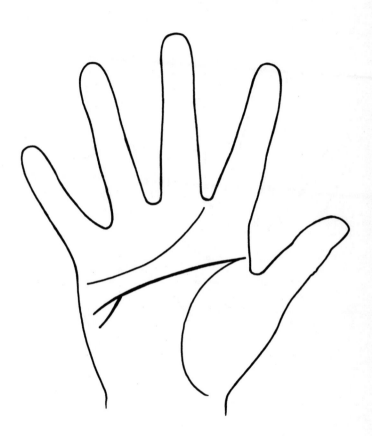

Figure 20: Writer's Fork

Figure 21: Head Line with Distinct Bend
at the End (Material Needs)

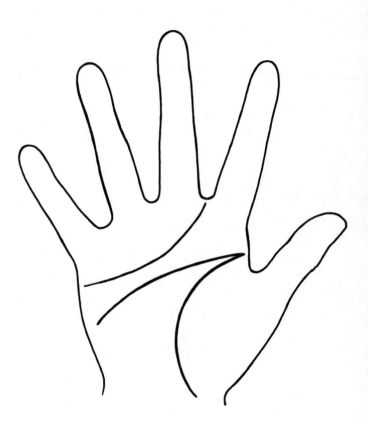

Figure 22: Head Line Joined to Life Line (Cautious)

Figure 23: Gap Between the Head and Life Lines
at the Start (Independence)

Life Line

The life line provides information on the person's physical well-being, health, and stamina. It also shows how enthusiastic the person is about his or her life.

There are more misconceptions about this line than about any other aspect of palmistry. I could not begin to estimate the number of times people have asked me whether their son's or daughter's short life line meant that they were going to die young. In fact, the life line has little or no bearing on length of life, and short life lines usually lengthen as the person ages.

The life line shows the degree of vitality and energy the person has at any time in his or her life. It also shows how enthusiastic and passionate the person is. Consequently, it is strongly related to the degree of pleasure the person gets out of life.

Although I do not read this line first, it is by far the most important line on the hand, since it clearly shows the amount of life and energy the person has at every stage of his or her life.

The life line starts on the side of the hand between the Jupiter (first) finger and thumb. It then sweeps in a semicircle around the thumb, ending close to the base of the palm, near the wrist.

The amount of area it encircles is important. A life line that comes well across the palm reveals someone with a great deal of stamina and energy (figure 24). This person will be adventurous, take chances, and make the most of every opportunity. A life line that closely hugs the thumb belongs to someone who is half alive, listless, and lacking in energy and enthusiasm (figure 25).

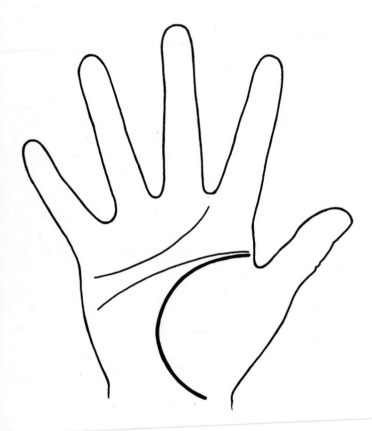

Figure 24: Life Line Coming Well Across the Palm (Energy)

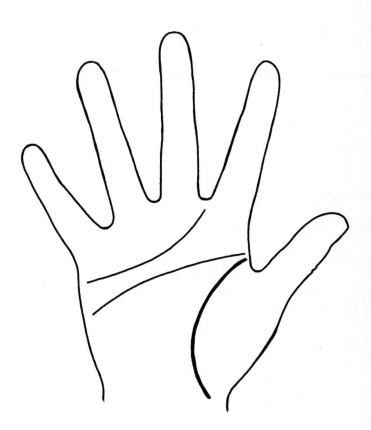

Figure 25: Life Line That Hugs the Thumb
(Lacking in Energy)

The raised mound encircled by the life line is known as the mount of Venus, and determines how passionate the person is. The mound should be raised and feel slightly firm to the touch. The higher it is, the more passionate the person will be. If it is spongy to the touch, the person will be interested in sensual pleasures and will overindulge whenever the opportunity arises.

I have seen mounts of Venus that are inverted. People with this formation have no interest in sex and usually dislike people of the opposite sex. They are inclined to be cold and unfeeling.

The starting position of the life line is important. With most people it starts approximately halfway between the base of the first finger and the thumb. (This, incidentally, is the perfect position for it to start, since in palmistry we are always looking for balance.) If the life line starts closer to the first finger than this, the person will be ambitious and determined to achieve his or her goals. This trait becomes more pronounced the closer to the first finger the life line begins. Conversely, if the life line starts close to the thumb, the person will be lacking in ambition and take life exactly as it comes.

The life line itself should be deep, clear, and well marked. Someone with a line like this will enjoy good health and be passionate about life. Most life lines are a mixture. The line might be well marked for part of its length and then become fainter for a while before becoming strong again. The faint period marks a time when the person's energy levels were lower than usual. This is likely to have been a period of ill health.

Islands on the life line reveal depression at the time indicated. They can also indicate a period of hospitalization. A chained life line is an indication of numerous health problems, usually of an emotional nature.

Breaks on the life line are common and are usually periods when the person changes his or her outlook on life. Sometimes, though, these breaks can be dramatic, and are usually caused by a relationship breakdown or a health problem. Usually, any break will be covered by an overlap of the line, which provides a form of protection at the time indicated. The overlap becomes a small "sister line."

Sister Line

A sister line is a fine line on the thumb side of the life line (figure 26). It is called a sister line since it parallels the life line, becoming in effect a "sister" to it. It is also known as the line of Mars. Some people have a sister line that covers the entire length of the life line. Usually though, it is found at the start of the life line, covering the growing up years. The sister line is rather like having two life lines and provides additional protection for the person at the times indicated. If someone has a sister line near the end of his or her life line, for instance, this person will be protected in later life and will not end up bedridden or incapacitated. A sister line is always a fortunate line to see on a hand.

Worry Lines

Many people have a series of fine lines that radiate out from the base of the thumb towards the life line, sometimes even crossing it (figure 27). These are known as

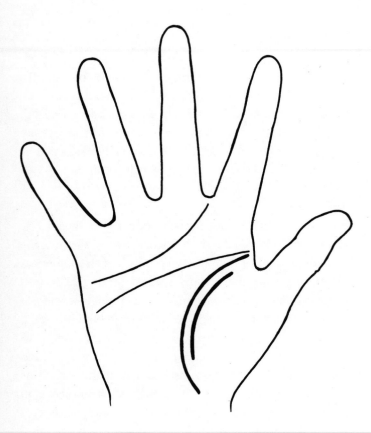

Figure 26: Sister Line (Also Known as the Line of Mars)

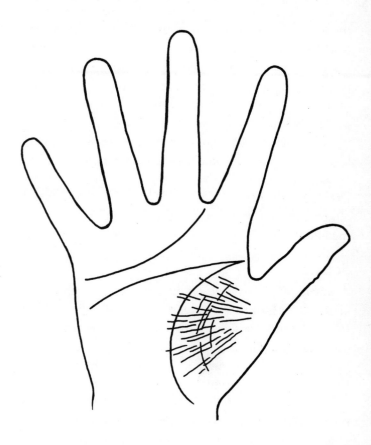

Figure 27: Worry Lines

worry lines. Some people have very few of these, while other people have hundreds. Most people worry about things that never happen, and the person with hundreds of worry lines will worry incessantly about virtually everything. Interestingly, it is common for such a person to be married to a partner who has very few of these lines. Obviously, he or she does not need to worry at all, since the partner is doing enough worrying for both of them!

Most worry lines are not of great importance, but worry lines that cross the life line have the potential to affect the person's health. Obviously, you can not give advice if these lines are in the person's past, but if they are in the future, I always mention them and suggest that the person learn meditation or self-hypnosis to enable them to worry less.

Squares

A square on the life line can be positive or negative. If it straddles the life line and covers a break in the line, it is said to be a "protective square" (figure 28). As the name indicates, this provides strength, support, and protection at a time when the person needs it. It shows that the person will have enough energy to successfully handle the situation.

A square that straddles the life line but is not covering a break indicates a period of confinement. This could mean a period of time spent in a closed society, such as a monastery. However, it usually means a period of time in prison. I may or may not mention this if I see it in the person's past. It depends purely on the circumstances and the reasons why I am giving the reading. Often a square such as this is a result of a youthful indiscretion and nothing is

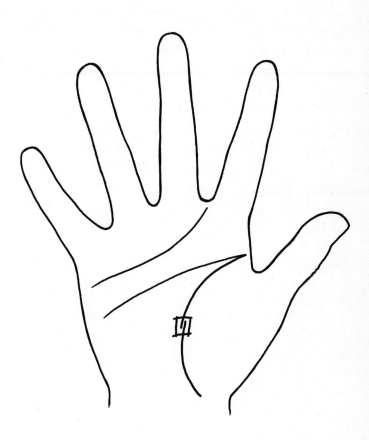

Figure 28: Protective Square

served by mentioning it. However, I almost always mention it, if it is in the future. I also tell the person that he or she has the power to change his or her destiny, and that the square can disappear from the palm before the person reaches it. The hand is a map of potentials and is always changing.

Destiny Line

The destiny line provides the vehicle through which the heart, head, and life lines express themselves.

Everyone has a heart, head, and life line. Not everyone has a destiny line. The destiny line is roughly in the middle of the palm, starting near the wrist and running towards the fingers (figure 29). It is complicated by the fact that it can start anywhere near the base of the hand, and finish close to any of the fingers. However, most destiny lines start close to, or even touching, the life line and head towards the second finger.

It is complicated further by the fact that some people's destiny lines do not start until they are in their twenties or thirties. As the destiny line crosses the head line at the age of thirty-five, some people's destiny lines start near the head line. When this situation occurs, it shows that the person did not know what to do with his or her life until reaching the age where the destiny line began.

Just recently I noticed that one of my son's history lecturers at college had a destiny line that started close to his wrist. Both of his parents were teachers, and he grew up wanting to follow in their footsteps. It is unusual to find a destiny line that is uniformly clear and well marked throughout its length.

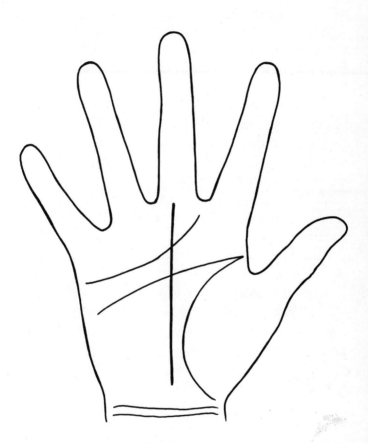

Figure 29: Destiny Line

Other people have destiny lines that are strong for a while, but then fade or even disappear for a time before returning. This shows that the person knew what he or she was doing for a period of time, but then went through a stage where he or she was drifting aimlessly, without a sense of direction.

The destiny line gives a sense of purpose to the person's life. The most fortunate people are those who decide at an early age what they want to do with their lives, and then go out and make it happen. These people will always have a strong, clear, well-marked life line.

Most people have no real idea of what they want to do with their lives. Consequently, the periods in their lives when their destiny line is strong and well marked indicate the times when they knew where they were going, and were working hard to achieve whatever their goal or dream was.

All good athletes have strong destiny lines. Obviously, to succeed in any highly competitive field, you have to be motivated, determined, and focused. A strong destiny line provides all of these qualities.

The presence of a destiny line means that, generally speaking, the person is protected and will usually manage to make the right decision or do the right thing.

In the past, palmists believed that the presence of a long destiny line guaranteed success. However, people also need to be motivated to become successful. A lazy person with a long destiny line will achieve only a fraction of what he or she is capable of, because there is no deep desire to be successful. I have seen many beggars in India with long, well-marked destiny lines. This does not mean success. It simply means that they have followed the same career right through life.

It used to surprise me whenever I read the palms of a successful person who did not have a destiny line. People without a destiny line often lead interesting and varied lives. They drift from one thing to another, taking life pretty much as it comes. I have read the palms of many misfits, criminals, and people who suffer from addictions of all sorts who do not have a destiny line.

Consequently, it is comparatively unusual to meet a highly successful person without a destiny line. Often, as they become successful, a line will form to show that the person has finally worked out the future direction of his or her life.

At one stage in my life I was a pitchman demonstrating products at fairs and shows. I enjoyed the fact that I would work incredibly hard for the time the show was on, and then have a week or two off before starting again. I found it fascinating that most of my fellow pitchmen lacked a destiny line. They enjoyed the lifestyle and the fact that they could sell a certain product for as long as they wished and then switch to selling something else. They might sell saucepans for six months, and then switch to knives or ballpoint pens. The lack of a destiny line revealed their interesting and unorthodox path through life. Highly successful sales people usually have strong, well-marked destiny lines. However, they focus on a specific career and follow it through. My pitchmen friends only worked as hard as they needed to to make ends meet.

Some authorities refer to the destiny line as the "fate line." I do not like this name as it appears to indicate that our lives are preordained, and we are simply puppets dancing while fate pulls the strings. I believe that we have the power to change our lives. Indeed, I have seen this many times on people's hands. In *Revealing Hands* I told the story of a man whose hands showed that he was going to spend most of his life in prison. However, he changed his way of thinking, turned his life around, and is now leading a happy and successful life.[1]

Starting Positions

The destiny line usually starts close to, or joined to, the life line. This usually means that the person was brought up in a close family environment. He or she would have been taught right from wrong, and would have had someone to turn to when things were not going well.

If the destiny line starts away from the life line, approximately halfway across the palm, the person would have had a more independent start in life (figure 30). This could be caused by a number of factors. Maybe the person's family members were not close, and the child had to learn to stand on his or her own two feet at an early age. Perhaps the child was an orphan, or was sent away to boarding school.

If the destiny line starts more than halfway across the palm, we have a person who has always been strongly independent, and has never liked being told what to do.

If the destiny line starts well inside the passive-inner quadrant it is an indication that the person wants to achieve public recognition for his or her accomplishments.

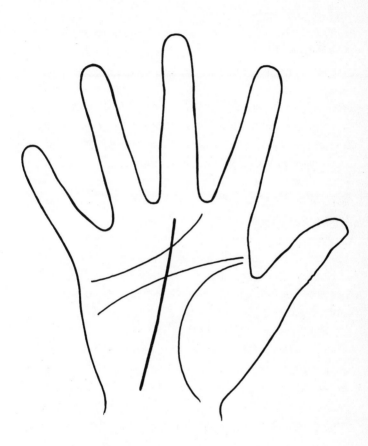

Figure 30: Destiny Line Starting Well Away from the Life
Line (Independent Outlook)

People with this type of destiny line have a need to be liked and appreciated by others.

Ending Positions

The ending position of the destiny line is extremely useful because it gives an indication of what the person enjoys doing. Most people's destiny lines end on or slightly beyond the heart line. The destiny line crosses the heart line at the age of forty-nine. If it stops on the heart line the person will become middle-aged and set in his or her ways. If the destiny line carries on beyond the heart line, the person will remain young at heart and will tackle new and different things all the way through life.

Most people's destiny lines end under the second finger, or between the second and third fingers. People with this ending position are likely to follow normal, orthodox careers. They might become bankers, teachers, or own a small business.

It is unusual for the destiny line to end under the first finger. People with this ending are likely to choose politics, philosophy, religion, or law as a career. This ending position is related to pride and ambition.

People who have a destiny line that ends under the third finger are happiest in a creative field. This could be art, literature, music, interior decorating, and any other career that utilized this interest. The lady who owns a florist shop near my home has a destiny line that almost touches her third finger. She worked as a secretary until she was in her mid-thirties, and then suddenly discovered what she was meant to be doing.

Occasionally, you will find a destiny line that crosses the palm diagonally and finishes below the little finger. Someone with this formation needs to use his or her voice to communicate. Entertainers and sales people are good examples. I once read the palm of a well-known stage actress who had a destiny line like this. She could express herself unbelievably well on stage, but was painfully shy and reserved when she was not performing. She told me that she lived only for the times when she was on stage, in front of an audience.

Double Destiny Line

Sometimes you will find people who have what appear to be two destiny lines that run parallel to each other for part of their length. The extra line is on the thumb side of the palm. This denotes someone who is capable of doing a number of tasks at the same time. This person might be just as involved in a hobby as she or he is in a career, or perhaps the career and home life are of equal importance. It is always a sign of versatility.

Other Factors

You will sometimes find a destiny line that has a distinct break in it. If the line stops and then starts again to one side of the original line, it is a sign of a change of direction. Often, these signs are seen only while the person is contemplating or doing the change. Once the change has been made, the two lines frequently join again to form a single destiny line.

For some years I sold printing machines. I was totally unsuited for this occupation, and stayed in it for as long as

I did only because it was extremely lucrative. During that time my destiny line had a distinct break in it. When I gave up the job and became a full-time psychic and teacher, my destiny line slowly turned into one distinct line again.

Occasionally, you will find a destiny line that veers away from its normal path and touches the life line before carrying on. This is a sign that family obligations took precedence over the individual's desires, and the person was not able to follow his or her dreams because of the needs of someone close.

Squares on the destiny line are a good sign and provide protection that shields the person from difficulties.

Now that we know something about the main lines, we will move on to determining timing in the hand, before covering the minor lines.

3

Timing on the Hand

For thousands of years palmists have argued about how to time events on the hand. I remember a heated discussion I had with several palmists in New Delhi thirty years ago, during which one gave another a black eye as they argued about how to time events. The rest of us agreed to differ, since we all had different ideas on the subject. In fact, there are a number of fundamental differences between Eastern and Western palmistry, and they were just as surprised to learn how I timed events on a hand as I was to learn their methods.

In practice, you have to look at both hands to determine the timing of important events. It is best if you can locate an important event that happened to the person in the past, and then measure backwards and forwards from that date.

Unfortunately, there is no automatic method that works every time. In the course of my practice, I have experimented with all of the methods that are described here.

However, I also use my intuition. I believe it is possible to become a capable palm reader without using any intuition at all. If you want to become an outstanding palmist, though, you must trust and act on your intuition.

I have a good example of this. Many years ago, shortly after I became a professional palmist, I was invited to read the palms of all the guests at a private party. I thoroughly enjoy bookings of this sort. The atmosphere is friendly and relaxed, and I have the opportunity to examine many hands in the course of the evening.

Unfortunately, this night I was not feeling well, and arrived at the party with a bad headache. I was placed in a dark corner to do the readings. I have learned to be prepared for any eventuality, and had a flashlight and magnifying glass with me.

However, when I began the first reading, I found that the concentration required made my headache worse. I thought that I would never get through the evening, but, far more quickly than I had expected, I had read everyone's palms, and was back home again. I managed to get rid of the headache in my sleep.

The next morning, the lady who had hosted the party phoned me. She was ecstatic about the readings I had given. Apparently, I had been incredibly specific and accurate about events that had happened in the past, and everyone had been extremely impressed. I was amazed. The whole evening had been a total blur for me. I was unable to focus and concentrate, and had done all the readings by saying the first thing that popped into my head.

Obviously, I was tuning in to my intuition, and by doing so had given better readings than usual, even with a bad headache. Ever since then, I have always said whatever pops into my mind, even though it may not make any sense to me. I may tell the client that it is an intuitive flash, and not something that I see in his or her palms. However, as I am holding and examining their hands, it is quite possible that I am obtaining the information through some form of psychometry.

It takes a great deal of practice to become good at timing events on a hand. Be patient. Try all the methods described here. Ask questions of your clients to determine how accurate you are. Gradually, you will find that you are becoming better and better at timing events in your clients' hands.

Be cautious of anyone who claims to be able to determine the actual month and day of a certain event. It is hard enough to determine the year accurately, and it is impossible to determine the day and month without using intuition. William G. Benham wrote: "There are some who can tell of an event and fix the time within a year, but those who have reached such skill are few. Others are successful within two, three, or five years. No one can do more than fix the year in which such an event occurs, if he relies entirely upon the rules of Palmistry."[1]

Destiny Line

By far the easiest way to determine timing is to use the destiny line (figure 31). It takes the first thirty-five years of the person's life for the destiny line to reach the head line. It takes the next fourteen years to reach the heart line (at age

forty-nine), and the rest of the life is taken up with what-ever part of the destiny line remains. Consequently, the first part of the destiny line, up to where it meets the head line, can be divided into three, giving the approximate ages of twelve and twenty-four. Likewise, the section between the head and heart lines can be divided in half, to give the age of forty-two.

It may seem strange that the first thirty-five years of life take up the bulk of the destiny line. This is because it is the time when we are growing up and working out what we want to do with our lives. By the age of thirty-five, most people have a reasonably clear idea of what they want to do. However, I have a friend of eighty-three who is still try-ing to work out what he wants to do with his life!

Between the ages of thirty-five and forty-nine the per-son is usually following a stable path. He or she is likely to be in a permanent relationship and progressing in a career. Obviously, if this is the not the case, there will be changes in the destiny line between the head and heart lines.

It may seem strange that most people's destiny lines stop at around the age of forty-nine. It certainly does not mean that they have no destiny after that age. All it means is that most people are set in their ways by that time, and, conse-quently, there are no great changes of direction in their fifties, sixties, or seventies.

People with a destiny line that carries on well beyond the heart line will experience new and different activities in later life. This could be a sign of a late starter, in many cases. It is often an indication of longevity.

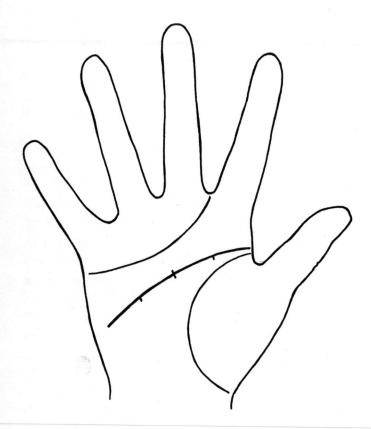

Figure 32: Timing Using the Head Line

Head Line

The head line usually shows about seventy years of life (figure 32). Naturally, if the person gets beyond that age, the head line will grow to reflect that. However, if you are reading the palms of someone who is less than, say, sixty years old, you can divide the head in life in half, to give the age of thirty-five. Naturally, each half can be divided again and again, to make the measurements as precise as you wish.

Life Line

The most accurate timing can be done using the life line. The simplest method is to divide the life line in two, by imagining a line running down the middle of the second finger and down the palm until it touches the life line. This is approximately the age of thirty-five. In fact, this system can also provide two other ages. An imaginary line running down the middle of the first finger and onto the palm reaches the life line at the age of ten. A similar line beginning from between the first and second fingers reaches the life line at the age of twenty (figure 33).

You can use these basic divisions for more precise timing. For instance, the age of seventy is where the life line curves back around the thumb at the base of the hand. The distance between the imaginary line marking the age of thirty-five and the position where the life line starts to go back around the thumb is a period of thirty-five years. If you divide this part of the life line in two, you will be at the age of fifty-two and a half. Dividing it in three gives you the ages of almost forty-seven and fifty-nine. You can keep on dividing indefinitely to get more and more precise with

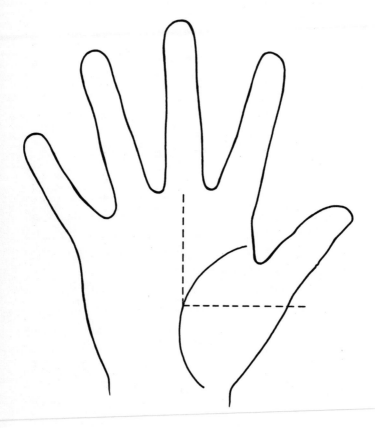

Figure 33: Timing Using the Life Line

your timing. In practice, if I wanted to be absolutely specific, I would take a palm print of the hand and then use
mathematical dividers for total accuracy.

In the past, people died much younger than we do
today. The biblical age of "threescore and ten" is not considered to be old nowadays. Consequently, this has to be
taken into account with any method of determining time
from the life line.

Desbarrolles' Method

Using mathematical dividers is similar to the ancient
method described by Adolphe Desbarrolles (1801–86) in
his influential book *Les Mystères de la main*.[2] He suggested
placing one point of a compass in the center of the base of
the Jupiter finger, and the other at the center of the base of
the Apollo finger. Describe a circle until the compass point
reaches the life line. This marks a period of ten years. Now
place the compass point that was on Apollo between the
Apollo and Mercury fingers and describe another circle.
This one marks out twenty years. After this extend the
compass out to the outermost part of the base of the Mercury finger and make another circle. This one marks forty
years. Next the free point of the compass is placed on the
heart line at the point it reaches the top of the palm. The
circle created marks fifty years. I have found that this system works only with people who have average life lines. If
the life line either hugs the thumb or comes well across the
palm, this system is worthless. This method also devotes far
too much space for the first ten years of life.

Desbarrolles learned this method from the Gypsies and used it for some forty years, before deciding that it was not accurate enough. In his monumental book, *Révélations complètes*,[3] he was brave enough to admit that this ancient method did not work. It is interesting to reflect that perhaps this system did work thousands of years ago, but the shapes of our hands have altered so much since then that this method is no longer valid.

Life Line Two

Another method of timing is to measure the length of the life line from where it begins to where it starts to turn back around the thumb. The age at this point is about seventy. Once we have this length, we can determine any age we want. For instance, half of that length will be thirty-five.

Some people have life lines that go right around the thumb and finish only because the skin patterns end. This is generally considered to indicate one hundred years of life. However, you must remember that by doing this we are only measuring periods of time. A long life line is no guarantee that the person will live to a ripe old age.

A third method is to mentally divide the life line into three equal sections from where it begins to about the age of seventy. Each section marks out twenty to twenty-five years.

Another method is to determine an important event on the person's life line. A serious event, such as an illness or accident, is usually shown clearly on the life line. By asking when that occurred, you will be able to date past and future events using it as a guide.

Some palmists feel that they should "see all, know all," and consequently do not ask questions. However, if by asking a question I can be more accurate and precise, I will certainly do so.

Occasionally, people come for a reading determined not to say a word, because they do not want to give the palmist any clues. I find this attitude rather strange, since we all reveal volumes about ourselves everywhere we go just through body language, and the palm itself invariably gives me all the information I need. I am happy to give readings to people who remain absolutely silent, but it takes longer to do a reading this way, and may not always cover the subjects they are especially interested in in great depth. By asking a few questions, I can both save time and be more helpful.

In India, it is common to use a piece of thread to determine timing. Some palmists in India prefer to use a hair from an elephant's tail—but these are not easy to find in the West! The thread is used to measure the distance from where the life line begins on the side of the palm to where it crosses on to the palmar surface. This represents seven years. The thread can then be used to measure seven year cycles all the way up the life line. This is similar to a method used by Cheiro, who also divided the life line into seven year periods.

The Henri Mangin Method

Henri Mangin was a famous French palmist, who published a number of books in the 1930s and 1940s. In his most famous book, *La Main, miroir du destin*,[4] he explained his system for determining time.

An imaginary line is drawn from the middle of the base of the Jupiter finger vertically to the life line. This indicates the age of ten. Another line, drawn from the middle of the Saturn finger reaches the life line at the age of forty. His system then becomes extremely complicated since it involves an imaginary line drawn from the start of the heart and life lines, and other lines going off this at an angle of forty-five degrees. I sometimes use his system for determining the ages ten and forty, but have had no success at using it to determine other ages. However, Henri Mangin used it successfully, as have several generations of French palmists.

Julius Spier

In Germany, many palmists date events from the wrist end of the life line. This is due to the influence of Julius Spier, the man who was responsible for Carl Jung's interest in palmistry. Julius Spier had an interesting method of determining time. He divided the life line into two. The first half (nearest the wrist in his system) represented the first twenty years of life. The other half was divided into two again, and the first half of this represented the ages twenty through to thirty. The remaining half is again divided into two to provide up to the age of forty, and the rest of the life line shows the remainder of the person's life. Unfortunately, Julius Spier died without explaining why he chose to date events from the wrist end of the life line.

I have had no success at all with Julius Spier's method, but include it for completeness.

As you can see, no one method is 100 percent accurate. However, even though these different methods sometimes seem to contradict each other, they have all worked for different people. Consequently, you should experiment with these different methods with an open mind. Ask questions and evaluate the results. You may find that one of these methods works perfectly for you, or you may find yourself using portions of a number of systems. It does not matter. Experiment, find the method that works best for you, and then practice until you become an expert.

In practice, I begin by dividing the life line in half (using the imaginary line running down the second finger). I then look for any important events that are shown on the life line to help me date things more accurately. Finally, I use the seven-year measurements that are used in India. I seldom use thread, but use my thumb and first finger to gauge the distance approximately. If I need even greater detail, I will use a piece of thread.

Finally, if I am trying to determine an event with as much accuracy as possible, I will take a palm print of the hand, and make all my measurements and calculations from that.

4

Minor Lines

There are a number of minor lines that also need to be looked at when reading a palm (figure 34). No one will have all of these lines. In fact, as mentioned earlier, some people have only three lines on their palms.

However, we do want minor lines on the hand. People who have only two, three, or four lines on their palms take life exactly as it comes and do not stop to pause, think, or reflect.

Obviously, when reading a palm, we do not look at every single line. Most of the smaller lines are caused by stress and tension. This is why a nervous, high-strung person will have many more lines on his or her hands than someone who is more relaxed and casual about life.

Girdle of Venus

The girdle of Venus (A) is a fine line that lies between the heart line and the fingers and parallels the heart line for part of its length. The presence of this line heightens the sensitivity and emotions of the person. This can sometimes create a

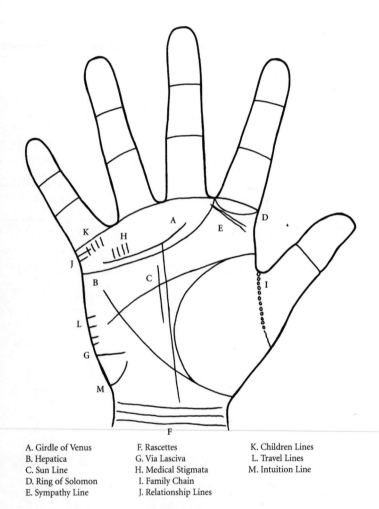

A. Girdle of Venus   F. Rascettes   K. Children Lines
B. Hepatica   G. Via Lasciva   L. Travel Lines
C. Sun Line   H. Medical Stigmata   M. Intuition Line
D. Ring of Solomon   I. Family Chain
E. Sympathy Line   J. Relationship Lines

Figure 34: The Minor Lines

difficult life because everything that happens will affect this person at an emotional level. People with this line benefit if they have some sort of creative outlet, because they can then channel their emotions into their creativity. People who do this often produce works of an extremely high standard.

Hepatica

The hepatica (B) is often known as the health line. It is also frequently known as the line of Mercury. The hepatica runs diagonally across the palm from inside the life line, close to the wrist, and crosses the palm to end close to the start of the heart line. It is not as clearly marked as the four major lines.

Interestingly, it is better not to have this line. People without a hepatica enjoy excellent health, and recover quickly from any illness.

If this line is present it should be clear and well marked. This is also a sign of good health and shows that the person is paying attention to his or her physical body.

The hepatica can also be an indication of longevity. When it virtually crosses the palm it is a sign that the person will pay attention to health matters and will probably outlast most of his or her contemporaries.

Most hepaticas show ups and downs in quality, indicating times of ill health. This need not necessarily be a disease. The person may simply be suffering from a loss of energy or a prolonged period of indifferent health.

Islands on the health line usually relate to digestive problems. I have seen a simple change in diet do wonders to the quality of people's health lines.

Breaks in the hepatica mark periods of ill health. This can usually be dated by looking for periods of weakness in the life line.

A square is a good sign to see on the health line. It means that the person is being protected during the period that the line is covered, and will enjoy a complete recovery from the illness or disease.

Sun Line

The Sun line (C) is a line that runs parallel to the destiny line for part of its length. It finishes close to, and under, the mount of Apollo. Consequently, it is frequently known as the line of Apollo. Ideally, it should be almost as long as the destiny line, but this is extremely rare. It usually starts close to the head line and runs up towards the third finger.

People blessed with a Sun line are confident, easy to get along with, and have the potential for great success. In fact, much of the time this line appears on the hand only after the person has decided what it is he or she wants to do and is working hard to achieve that goal.

Ring of Solomon

The ring of Solomon (D) is a semicircular line that surrounds the mount of Jupiter (see chapter 6) beneath the first (Jupiter) finger. This line gives the person an interest in psychic subjects. It also give the person an intuitive awareness of the needs of others and a desire to serve humanity in some sort of way. Not surprisingly, it usually gives a strong interest in psychology.

Sympathy Line

A sympathy line (E) is found in the same place as the ring of Solomon, immediately below the first finger. However, it is a straight line. People with this have a sympathetic, understanding outlook and approach to life.

Ring of Saturn

The ring of Saturn is a semicircular line that surrounds the mount of Saturn (see chapter 6) beneath the second (Saturn) finger. It is a negative indication that makes it virtually impossible for the person to achieve his or her goals. This can be extremely frustrating, since the person may be on the verge of success and then allow something insignificant to prevent it from happening.

The Rascettes

The rascettes (F), commonly known as the bracelets, are the lines on the wrist immediately below the palm. Gypsies claim that each full bracelet signifies twenty-five years of life. However, you will find that almost everyone has three bracelets. Consequently, they are ignored by most modern-day palmists. It is superstitious nonsense such as this that gave palmistry a bad name in the first place.

Although the rascettes are not taken into consideration for determining length of life, it is worth mentioning that for thousands of years palmists have known that when the top rascette of a woman's hand arches upwards into the palm she will have difficulties in childbirth. The ancient Greeks knew this, and women with this formation on their hands became vestal virgins at the temples and were not allowed to marry.

Via Lasciva

The via lasciva (G) is a straight line that runs part of the way across the palm, starting two-thirds to three-quarters of the way down the palm from the little finger, and heading across the palm towards the thumb. Occasionally this line is curved.

This line has had a bad reputation in the past and people who had it were believed to be lascivious and willing to overindulge in virtually anything. In fact, one book in my library says that people with the via lasciva in their hands have a "passionate thirst for money" and will lead a "life shortened by excesses."[1]

In fact, this line simply means that people who possess it have a strong need for something exciting to look forward to. They often have addictive personalities and need to keep away from alcohol and drugs. It is probably this tendency that gave the via lasciva such a bad name in the first place.

Medical Stigmata

The medical stigmata (H) is a group of three or four tiny vertical lines below the little finger. They are often found slightly offset towards the ring finger.

People with a medical stigmata have an empathy for all living things. Consequently, they make good gardeners, farmers, veterinarians, naturopaths, doctors, and nurses. In fact, they are happy in any career that involves helping others. Naturally, someone who went into one of these careers with the main aim of making money would not have a medical stigmata on his or her hand. Most people with it are everyday people who happen to be talented gardeners, good with animals, or have significant people skills. They might, for instance, know exactly the right words to say to help someone in distress. Whatever these people do, they receive immense satisfaction out of helping all living things. These fine lines are sometimes called "Samaritan lines."

Family Chain

The family chain (I) is a chain-like line that is found where the thumb joins the palm. (In the next chapter you will see that the family chain divides the second and third phalanges of the thumb.)

If this line is heavily chained, the person will have strong emotional ties with his or her family. Conversely, if this line is thin and unchained, the person will have a lack of emotional involvement with his or her family.

The family chain is read from the first finger side of the thumb. Frequently, you will find a line that is heavily chained at the start but gradually turns into a thin line. This shows that the person has gradually become less emotionally tied to his or her family.

Sometimes you will see a break in this line. This indicates a period of separation from the family.

Relationship Lines

Relationship lines (J) are fine lines that come up the side of the palm between the start of the heart line and the Mercury finger.

Relationship lines are frequently known as "marriage lines." This is not correct, since the presence of one or more relationship lines does not guarantee a marriage. In fact, these lines simply indicate a strong relationship, which may, or may not, be a sexual one.

I have met a number of married men who have no relationship lines on their hands. This means that the marriage is convenient and comfortable, but is not of great importance to them. I have never met a married woman who did not have a relationship line on her palm.

Ideally, the relationship lines should be clear, well marked and come up the side of the hand and on to the palmar surface. This is an indication of a major relationship that lasts for a long while. A strong line that does not come over the top is a sign of an important relationship that does not last.

The relationship lines indicate a potential. The presence of three or four lines does not necessarily indicate that number of strong relationships. If the first relationship is successful and lasts, the other lines will remain dormant and will not be utilized.

It is possible for these lines to disappear. If you have been in a strong relationship that ended badly, your subconscious mind can erase the line from your hand. However, the trauma will always be visible on your heart line. When you meet another person, a new relationship line will form.

Children Lines

The children lines (K) are fine vertical lines immediately below the Mercury finger. They sometimes overlap the relationship lines.

Once you start reading palms, you will be regularly asked, "How many children will I have?" One hundred years ago it was possible to answer that question, but it is not as easy nowadays.

Thanks to contraceptives we are able to choose when, or if, we will have children. Consequently, on a women's hand, the children lines show only a potential. She may choose to fulfill her potential, but nowadays most people have two or three children. Strong lines usually—but not always— show the number of children she has. The longer lines are said to indicate boys, and shorter lines girls. You will probably need to use a magnifying glass to determine that sort of information.

On a man's hand the children lines indicate children he is close to. Consequently, if a man has three children, but is close to only two of them, he will have just two children lines on his hand. This is further complicated by the fact that we can become close to other people's children. Consequently, a man who has never had children may have children lines on his hands. These could be the children of his partner, nieces or nephews, or any other children he is involved with.

Travel Lines

Travel lines (L) are the fine lines that come up the side of the hand between the wrist and the heart line on the Mercury finger side of the hand.

Although they are usually called "travel lines," a better name is "restlessness lines," since they give a degree of restlessness to the person's nature. Naturally, this inner restlessness frequently leads to travel, which is how these lines derived their name.

People with restlessness lines on their hand need change and variety. They dislike routine and regularity.

Strong lines represent important travel. Usually, the first major trip a person undertakes is considered the most important, and is most clearly marked. If someone travels regularly as part of his or her work, each individual trip would not be shown on the hand. However, this person would have a number of restlessness lines to indicate the desire for travel.

Naturally, an important trip varies from person to person. For someone who lived in a small village, miles from anywhere, a two hundred mile trip to a large city would be more important than a round the world trip taken by a business executive who flies somewhere every month.

Intuition Line

The line of intuition (M) starts on the little (Mercury) finger side of the hand, close to the wrist on the slightly raised mound (mount of Luna) at the base of the hand. It heads in an arc toward the center of the hand (plain of Mars).

Usually, this line is only half an inch or an inch long. However, when developed, it can extend down to join the head or destiny lines.

The presence of a line of intuition indicates that the person relies on his or her hunches and feelings. A well-developed line shows that the person has strong intuitive capabilities. He or she may be a natural clairvoyant, medium, or healer.

Naturally, it is possible for someone to be both a clairvoyant and healer. Usually, though, the person will be more talented in one area, than the other. If the line of intuition heads towards the head line, the person would make a natural healer. If it heads towards the destiny line, the person is more likely to be interested in telepathy, clairvoyance, and precognition.

Simian Crease

The simian crease (sometimes known as the "simian line") is created when the heart line and head line become a single line that runs across the palm (figure 35). Consequently, logic, and emotion become entwined in a single line. It is found frequently on one hand, but is seldom seen on both.

People with a simian line can be extremely agreeable and easy to get on with, but once their minds are made up, it is impossible to change them. They are inflexible, obstinate, and stubborn. Because the heart line (emotions) and head line (logic) are intertwined, these people find it extremely hard to express their feelings and have highly intense and complex emotional lives.

Figure 35: Simian Crease (Head and Heart Lines Combined)

If the simian crease is found only on the minor hand (the left hand if the person is right-handed) the person will have had a sheltered upbringing and will try to avoid responsibility.

When found on the major hand, the person will be a single-minded, hard-working achiever. However, he or she will also find it difficult to relax and take time off.

When found on both hands, the person will be unusually stubborn and rigid. This can create major difficulties, and people with it need careful direction and guidance from their parents from an early age. The enormous single-mindedness these people possess can be usefully utilized in sporting activities, and in a career that requires precision and little input from others.

People with a simian crease on both hands sometimes find it hard to distinguish right from wrong. Consequently, the person could become a master criminal or, with a slightly different upbringing, someone who helps humanity in some sort of way.

The simian crease is usually found in the hands of Down's syndrome sufferers. However, most people with it are perfectly normal and are usually highly intelligent.

5

The Fingers

Many people are surprised to find that the fingers have such an important part to play in palmistry. Most people tend to think the subject is concerned only with the lines on the palm, not realizing that you can tell a great deal from a simple glance at the fingers. For instance, someone who displays his or her palms with the fingers held apart will be more open and confident than someone who holds his or her fingers together. It is a sign of caution and timidity when the fingers are held together. When the fingers are held slightly apart it is an indication that the person is a reasonably independent thinker.

I have already mentioned how I decide which cashier to line up behind from the length of that person's fingers.

You already know something about the fingers. I explained in chapter 1 how long fingers denote patience and attention to details, while short fingers denote a faster, less detailed, and more impulsive approach.

Consequently, people with short fingers tend to become impatient with their longer-fingered colleagues because they like to jump in and get the job done as quickly as possible. They are enthusiastic and keen to start, but are not always as good at finishing. This is because their enthusiasm does not always last. They also frequently try to do too many tasks at the same time.

People with long fingers are virtually the opposite. They are patient and enjoy spending time thinking and planning about a task before commencing. They also like to take as much time as is necessary to successfully finish a task properly. They are conscientious, responsible, and methodical.

People with medium-length fingers combine the traits of the two extremes. Although they are usually responsible and conscientious, they might take shortcuts if the task does not appeal to them. They are usually patient, but might suffer from occasional outbursts of impatience.

Gaps Between the Fingers

How people hold their hands reveals a great deal about them. The gaps between the fingers are an extension of this. A noticeable gap between the first and second fingers, for instance, reveals someone who is confident and has good self-esteem. This person will stand up for what he or she believes in, and usually develops a strong faith or philosophy of life.

A noticeable gap between the second and third fingers is a sign of someone who lives for the moment, and has no concern or worry about what tomorrow will bring. This gap is extremely rare.

A noticeable gap between the ring and little finger is frequently found. This person is an independent thinker who likes to make up his or her own mind. It can also indicate someone who has problems in communication. This person may be able to talk confidently and at great length about matters that are not important, but will find it hard to express his or her emotions.

When the hand is held with all the fingers widely apart, the person is independent, carefree, friendly, and outgoing. He or she has nothing to hide.

When all the fingers are held together the person is cautious, reserved, and slow to make friends. This person is likely to constantly worry about what other people are thinking of him or her.

Ideally, we want a balance between having all the fingers held wide apart, and having them held together. A small space between each of the fingers indicates someone who is basically friendly, trusting, and independent in outlook.

The Fingertips

Fingertip shapes fit in well with d'Arpentigny's system of hand classification. They are generally square, spatulate, or conic. Most people have a mixture of these on their hands. People like this are versatile, adaptable, and have a wide range of interests. However, even when people contain a mixture of different types of fingertips, one type will predominate. They are likely to use this characteristic in their careers, and utilize the others in hobbies and other interests.

People with square fingertips are down-to-earth, capable, practical conformists. They are cautious, conservative, and methodical. They like to take time to mull things over before making decisions. They prefer the tried and true, and tend to dislike change.

People with conic fingertips are easygoing, sensitive, quick-thinking, and idealistic. They work best in pleasant surroundings and enjoy beauty in all its forms. They enjoy mentally stimulating conversations, but usually act on their feelings, rather than logic.

Every now and again you will come across someone with pointed fingertips. This is an extreme form of the conic. People with pointed fingertips are intuitive, inspirational, high-strung, and impressionable. These people find life hard to deal with, and are happiest inside a close relationship. However, they are overly possessive and frequently stifle their partners with a constant need for attention.

People with spatulate fingertips (tips that flare at the ends) are practical, intelligent, unconventional, inventive people who love new concepts and ideas. These people enjoy change and become extremely enthusiastic about new and different ways of doing things. They need challenges and work best when self-employed.

You will sometimes find people with droplets on the tips of their fingers. When the palm is held facing downwards, droplets can be seen like tiny drops of water on the tips of the fingers. People with droplets on their fingers are extremely sensitive and highly intuitive. They are caring, supportive people with a great love for all living things.

The Phalanges

Each finger is divided into three sections, known as phalanges. The first, or nail, phalange relates to spirituality and
intuition. Someone with long tip phalanges on each finger
will be thoughtful and interested in the spiritual side of life.

The middle phalange relates to the person's intellect.
People with long middle phalanges are generally successful
in business matters.

The base phalange relates to the material aspects of life.
People with long, thick, puffy base phalanges are self-indulgent and have a strong desire for physical gratification.

Base phalanges that are slightly spongy to the touch indicate someone who likes food and is usually a good cook.

Strain and Stress Lines

Indications of strain and prolonged stress show up clearly
on the fingers (figure 36). Fine, vertical lines on the base
phalange are indications of strain. They mean that the person has been overdoing things and would benefit by having
one or two days off. Even a good night's sleep can affect
these lines.

Much more serious than the strain lines are the stress lines.
These are fine, horizontal lines on the first, or nail, phalange
of the fingers. They reveal that the person has been suffering
stress and strain over a long period of time. These lines take
time to appear, and disappear just as slowly. Whenever I see
these lines I suggest that the person take a vacation, or
remove himself or herself from whatever situation is causing
the stress. Of course, this may not be easy, particularly if the
stress is caused by a relationship or work pressures.

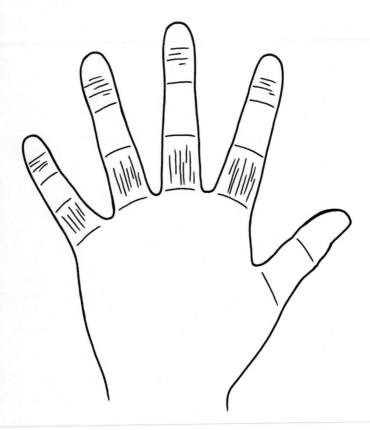

Figure 36: Stress and Strain Lines

If the stress continues, the stress lines move further down the fingers into the other phalanges. When this occurs, it is a sign that the person's health is in danger of being affected as a result of the continued stress.

Straight and Crooked Fingers

Ideally, all of the fingers should be straight. When they curve towards the fingers on either side, it means that the person is subconsciously underrating himself or herself in the area indicated by the curved finger, and is gaining support from the other fingers.

Occasionally, you will find a little finger that appears to be twisted. You need to be careful with the interpretation of this since it can be an inherited trait. However, it can also be a sign of potential dishonesty. Be careful with any financial dealings you may have with these people. I have noticed this strange formation on the little fingers of many moneychangers at the railway stations in India.

Knotty and Smooth Fingers

Fingers are considered to be either smooth or knotty. Knotty fingers are those where the joints are extremely visible. People with knotty joints in their fingers like to analyze everything, taking very little on trust or face value. People with smooth fingers are more trusting and intuitive.

In my classes, I would have my students imagine ideas coming into the body through the fingertips. Every time these thoughts reached a knotty joint, they would go round and around in a process of examination and analysis before continuing. Consequently, ideas and thoughts enter the palms of smooth-fingered people much more quickly than they do with people with knotty joints. If you know someone who likes to analyze and discuss the smallest detail for hours on end, you can be sure that this person will have knotty fingers.

Not surprisingly, knotty joints are found frequently on the fingers of people with philosophical hands.

The knots between the first and second phalanges are known as the "knots of mental order." People with these are logical, methodical, and mentally alert. They invariably act on logic rather than intuition.

The knots between the second and third phalanges are called "knots of material order." These people overanalyze everything, and this can inhibit their creative potential. People who have knots of material order on their fingers almost always have an abundance of worry lines on their palms as well.

Setting of the Fingers

The fingers can be set on the hand in four different ways. The most usual formation is that of a gently curved arch, in which the first and fourth fingers are set slightly below the second and third fingers (figure 37). This denotes a well-balanced person who is fair, easy to get along with, and does not consider himself or herself superior or inferior to anyone else.

When the first and fourth fingers are set considerably lower than the second and third fingers we have what is known as a tented arch formation. People with this particular setting are lacking in confidence and have considerable

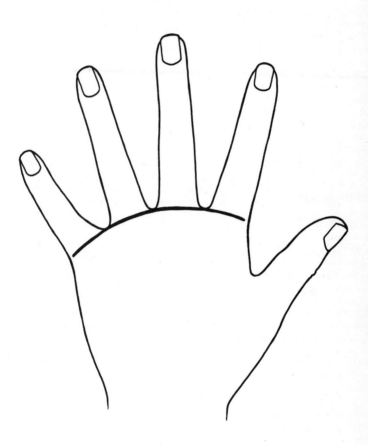

Figure 37: Fingers Set on a Curved Arch
(Well-Balanced Person)

doubts about their abilities. They lack self-esteem and feel that they are not in control of their own lives.

When the fingers are all arranged in a straight line we have someone who is confident and proud of his or her capabilities and achievements. If the first and second fingers are also equal in length this person will be vain, ruthless, arrogant, and condescending to others.

The "dropped" little finger is a setting that is frequently found today. It occurs when the first three fingers are set in a gentle curve, but the little finger is set considerably lower than the others (figure 38). This is an indication that the person will have to learn the hard way, usually through disappointments and setbacks. Everything will go well for a long time and then, usually quite suddenly, this person will find himself or herself in a difficult situation that will take a great deal of time and effort to resolve.

Flexibility

If the fingers are supple, the person will have a flexible mind. He or she will frequently act on intuition and will be open to all points of view. In extreme cases, where the fingers appear to be virtually double-jointed, the person will be excitable and love talking (usually about himself or herself).

Conversely, if the fingers appear hard and rigid, with no flexibility whatsoever, the person will also be rigid and fixed in his or her outlook and approach.

Fingernails

Subliminally, we all notice fingernails and make assessments based on their condition. We assume that someone

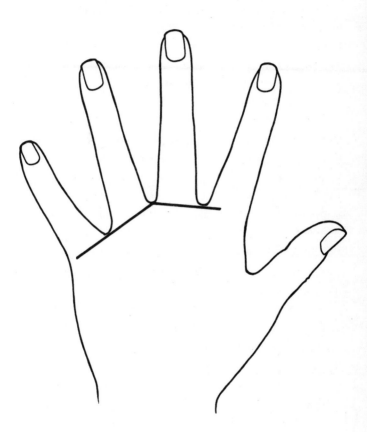

Figure 38: Fingers Set on a Tented Arch (Lack of Confidence)

with manicured fingernails will be refined and cultured, just as we assume the opposite about someone with dirty, broken, or uncut fingernails.

One of my regular customers at a bookstore I owned many years ago always tried to conceal her bitten nails when paying for her books. She was embarrassed about her nervous habit. However, what she found hardest to deal with was the fact that people immediately lowered their expectations of her as soon as they saw her nails. I encouraged her to visit a hypnotherapist to cure her of the habit. As soon as her fingernails grew, her self-esteem and confidence increased dramatically.

Fingernails vary greatly. Ideally, they should follow the shape of the finger.

The ideal fingernail is wide and medium in length. It should be slightly longer than it is wide. People with nails like this are energetic, faithful, and honest.

People with long fingernails are sensitive and emotional. They enjoy creative activities.

If the fingernails are narrow, as well as long, the person is inclined to be selfish and always wants to get his or her own way. Narrow fingernails are always a sign of a narrow-minded person who is fixed in his or her ways.

People with short fingernails are hard on themselves and suffer from nervous tension. They are impatient and inclined to be critical.

If the nail is short and narrow, and looks small compared to the fingertip, the person will be frugal, mean, and avoid spending money if it can possibly be avoided. This person takes pride in being parsimonious.

Vertical ridges on the fingernail can be caused by either a deficiency in the diet or extreme nervousness.

Horizontal ridges are caused by illness or stress at the time that the nail was first becoming visible.

White dots on the nails are caused by stress and anxiety. They can also indicate a calcium deficiency.

The color of the nails can also give a clue to the health of the person. The ideal nail appears pinkish in color and contains no ridges or white spots on it. Red fingernails belong to people who become overexcited or agitated very easily. A nail that appears white is likely to belong to someone who is anemic. Liver problems are indicated when the nails have a yellowish tinge. A blue tinge to the nails reveals circulation problems. If the nails have always had a bluish hue, the person is likely to be cold and unfriendly.

The Jupiter Finger

Keywords: ambition, independence, confidence, faith, and philosophy

The Jupiter finger is the first finger and denotes pride, ambition, leadership, and the ego. In palmistry we are always looking for balance. Consequently, we want this finger to be approximately the same length as the third finger (figure 39). It is usually easier to determine the relative lengths of the first and third fingers by looking at the back of the hand.

If the first finger is noticeably longer than the third finger, the person will be self-motivated and have a strong desire to be successful. In normal circumstances, this is a good quality. However, many people with this trait do not know when to stop, and push themselves into an early grave.

If the first finger is noticeably shorter than the third finger the person will lack confidence in early life. He or she will be inclined to hold back, rather than push forward. This means that in the growing up years this person can be pushed around by others, and will find it hard to stand up for himself or herself. However, in later life, a Jupiter finger that is shorter than the third one can be an advantage, since this person will know when to pause and relax, and when to push forward.

When the first and third fingers are roughly equal in length, the person will be reasonably ambitious, but will know when to pause and relax. He or she will be realistic in outlook and will not waste time pursuing unrealistic dreams.

The first finger should be straight. If it curves towards the second finger the person will be self-centered, self-pitying, and lacking in confidence. It is a sign of low self-esteem. He or she will need constant support and encouragement.

The phalanges should be approximately equal in length. If the tip phalange is the longest, the person will have strong religious or philosophical interests. He or she will enjoy working with others who think along similar lines.

If the middle phalange is the longest, the person will have a practical and positive approach towards life. He or she is likely to possess a keen intelligence.

The base phalange is the one that is most likely to be the longest on the Jupiter finger. This gives the person a strong interest in philosophy and religion. Some people with this combination take up the church as a career, but for most,

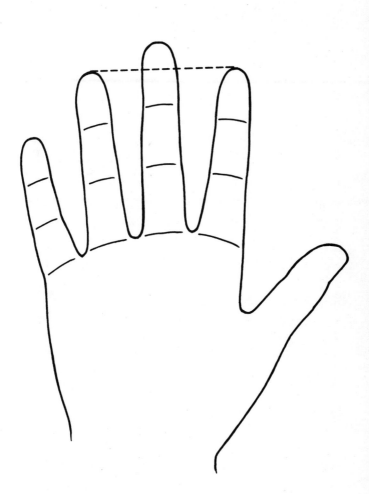

Figure 39: Jupiter Finger Same Length as Apollo Finger

it provides a questioning sort of faith that these people gradually build up and develop as they go through life.

You will sometimes see a Jupiter finger that has an extremely short base phalange. People with this on their hands are happiest when left to their own devices. They are modest, self-deprecating, and devoid of ambition.

The Saturn Finger

Keywords: responsibility, limitations, and common sense

The second finger is named after Saturn, the Roman god of agriculture. He was a rather gloomy god who gave his name to the word "saturnine." Consequently, this finger relates to duty, service, restrictions, restraint, and common sense.

The second finger should be the longest finger on the hand. If it is too long, in comparison with the other fingers, the person will be happiest on his or her own, and will need very little contact with other people. If this finger is too short in comparison with the other fingers the person will lack any sense of responsibility. In practice, most people have Saturn fingers that are neither too long nor too short.

The Saturn finger should be straight. However, it is the finger that is most likely to curve one way or the other. If it curves towards the first (Jupiter) finger, the person will underrate himself or herself, and be overly deprecating and nervous. A curve in this direction is often a sign of an inferiority complex (especially when the Jupiter finger is shorter than the third finger).

If the Saturn finger curves over the third (Apollo) finger, the person will be holding himself or herself back creatively, and will need a great deal of encouragement from others.

People with this formation are usually aware of their capabilities, but prefer to dabble, rather than run the risk of failing if they work too hard or take the task seriously.

The Saturn finger is often held close to one of the adjacent fingers when the hand is held open. This is known as a "finger cling."

If the Saturn finger almost touches the third finger when the hand is held open, the person will have a strong interest in the arts and would be happiest working in some creative field.

If this finger almost touches the Jupiter finger it is a sign that the person will eventually be in an influential position in his or her career.

Of course, it also means something when the Saturn finger stands on its own and does not curve or cling to an adjacent finger. This is an indication that any influence the person manages to achieve will come from outside his or her career.

Naturally, we want the phalanges to be approximately equal in length. If the tip phalange is longer than the others, the person will be cautious, conservative, and proud of his intellect. He or she is likely to feel superior to people who are less well endowed. If the tip phalange is extremely long, at the expense of the other two phalanges, the person will be gloomy, sad, and melancholy—in fact, saturnine.

The middle phalange is the one that is most likely to be longest. This denotes someone who is a good organizer and enjoys detailed work. He or she will be conscientious and methodical. When the finger is smooth, without obvious joints, a long middle phalange gives an interest in the occult.

If the middle phalange is extremely short, compared to the other two phalanges, the person will dislike work and will fritter his or her time away, and achieve little.

A long base phalange gives an interest in agriculture, which is probably why this finger was named after Saturn, the god of agriculture. People with this formation enjoy working with the soil, and make good gardeners, farmers, and people who enjoy being out of doors.

The Apollo Finger

Keywords: creativity, self-expression, and aesthetic sense

The third finger is known as the "Apollo" or "Sun" finger. It represents beauty, refinement, and creativity. An average length Apollo finger reaches halfway up the fingernail of the Saturn finger, and is about the same length as the Jupiter finger. If it is longer than this, the person will have an aesthetic, creative nature that needs to be expressed in some sort of way. If this finger is extremely long (almost the same length as the Saturn finger), the person will be reckless and take risky chances that most people would refuse. Often, this formation creates an interest in gambling.

Naturally, the Apollo finger should be as straight as possible. If it curves toward the Saturn finger it is an indication that the person has a creative talent that has been put to one side while the person focuses on something more mundane. You will find this formation on the hands of many creative people who are not able to make a living out of their creativity, and are forced to do other work.

When the Apollo finger curves toward the little finger it reveals that the person is subconsciously underrating his or her creative ability. An acquaintance of mine is a talented potter who is never satisfied with what he produces. Behind his pottery studio is a small mountain of discarded items that he feels are not good enough to sell. His Apollo finger has a pronounced curve toward the little finger.

It is usual for all the phalanges to be the same length on this finger. People with this combination enjoy nice things and work best in pleasant surroundings.

When the tip phalange is longer than the others the person will have high ideals, and frequently display a creative talent. Whenever I see a long tip phalange on this finger I immediately look at the person's head line to see if it curves towards the wrist (indicating a good, creative imagination).

The second phalange is the one that is most likely to be the longest on the Apollo finger. It indicates natural good taste, and the ability to use it in a career. Someone with this formation would be brilliant at selling items that he or she personally found to be attractive, but would be unable to sell anything that he or she disliked.

It is unusual for the base phalange to be longer than the others. It indicates a totally materialistic approach to life with little interest in aesthetic or cultural activities. When they become successful these people like to surround themselves with expensive, often gaudy, objects to impress others.

The Mercury Finger

Keywords: communication, business and finance, and quick thinking

Mercury was the Roman messenger of the gods. Consequently, the fourth finger relates to communication. It is also related to commerce and sex.

An average length little finger reaches up to about the first joint of the third finger. The longer this finger is, the better the person is at communication. People with short little fingers find it hard to express themselves. If the finger is extremely short, the person will remain emotionally immature, and this will reveal itself in many different ways. It frequently reveals itself in relationship and sexual problems.

However, before assessing the length of the finger you have to see how it is set on the palm. As mentioned earlier, many people have a "dropped" little finger, and this may make the finger appear shorter than it actually is. In these instances, you have to mentally set this finger alongside the others to determine if it is short, long, or average in length.

It is important for this finger to be straight, since this is a sign of honesty. When it is bent or twisted, it shows that the person is potentially dishonest. A man who used to work at our local post office had a twisted little finger. I quickly discovered that I had to check my change after dealing with him, since it was never correct. Whenever I see a twisted little finger on someone's hand, I stress the necessity of being careful and honest in all business dealings.

It is rare for the three phalanges on the Mercury finger to be even in length. The tip phalange is almost always the longest. Since this section governs verbal communication, this phalange is invariably long in people who make their livelihoods using their voice. Teachers, entertainers, and sales people are obvious examples.

When the tip phalange is short the person will find it hard to express himself or herself, and will appear shy and retiring.

The middle phalange is usually small. This section relates to written communication, and most people tend to avoid this whenever possible. People with large middle phalanges are good at expressing themselves with words on paper. They may not necessarily like doing it, but have a definite talent in this direction. You will find this formation on the hands of professional writers, of course, but you will also find it on people who are good at writing letters, or can express things more clearly by writing them down, rather than saying them out loud.

The base phalange relates to money, finance, and business. Someone with this formation will love money, and will be inclined to bend the truth when necessary to obtain it.

The Mercury finger sometimes curves towards the Apollo finger. This formation is known as the "finger of sacrifice," and shows that the person will give up his or her own ambitions to help others. This formation is most likely to be found on the hands of caregivers, and people who are involved in the healing professions.

The Thumb

Keywords: logic, willpower, reasoning ability, independence, and vitality

The thumb plays an important role in palmistry. Many palmists, particularly in India, pay more attention to the thumb than any other part of the hand. This is because it clearly reveals the person's character.

Only primates have opposing thumbs. Our thumbs contain a radial nerve that is made of the same nerve fiber that runs through our spinal columns and is also found in the middle of our brains. This radial nerve gives us the superior reasoning capabilities that enabled us to rise so far above the rest of the animal kingdom.

Speaking generally, the larger the thumb, the greater the degree of success the person will enjoy in life. Napoleon is believed to have had an extremely large thumb. Obviously, other factors need to be looked at, as well. Someone with a large thumb, but no motivation or energy, will not amount to much. However, the large thumb would still enable him or her to achieve much more than would have been the case if it had not been present.

People with large thumbs are generally motivated, persistent, and ambitious. They also have leadership qualities. All of this enables them to achieve their goals.

People with short thumbs are generally easygoing. They can be obstinate and stubborn on occasion, but lack will.

Most people have thumbs of average length. These reach at least halfway up the base phalange of the Jupiter finger. People with average thumbs can stand up for themselves when required and have a sense of fair play.

The setting of the thumb can sometimes make it hard to determine if it is short, medium, or long. When the thumb is set high up on the hand towards the fingers, the person will be original, outgoing, and adventurous. When the thumb is set low down towards the wrist the person will be cautious and think carefully before acting. Most people have thumbs that are set neither high nor low.

Most people's thumbs are held at an angle of about forty-five degrees to the hand. This shows that they are reasonably broad-minded, but still conform to society's expectations and standards. The wider the angle of the thumb, the more outgoing and generous the person will be. It can be an interesting exercise to watch people's thumbs on television. You will find a large number of entertainers with a wide angle of the thumb.

People with a small angle of the thumb are inclined to be small-minded, selfish, and negative. They are usually concerned only with their immediate family and have little interest in anything else.

There are two angles, or bumps, that can be found on the thumb. The first of these is the angle of practicality, which is an angle, or bulge, on the outside of the thumb at the bottom of the second phalange. As its name indicates, people with this angle are good with their hands and often enjoy careers that are "hands on." The larger the angle, the greater the practicality.

This angle is sometimes known as the "angle of time." It does not necessarily mean punctuality, but someone with this formation will invariably be at the right place at the right time. This formation can be extremely useful to a comedian, for instance, because it will give him or her a good sense of timing.

Some people have no angle at this position. These people are not manually dexterous, and would do better in a field that utilized their heads more than their hands.

The other angle on the thumb is called the "angle of pitch." It is found at the base of the thumb where it joins the wrist. This angle gives the person a good ear for music and a natural sense of rhythm.

Many entertainers have both of these angles on their thumbs. This means that they have a good sense of timing, a good ear for music, and a natural sense of rhythm.

The thumb is divided into three phalanges (figure 40). Two of these are obvious, but the third is not. It comprises the mound, or mount, immediately below the thumb that is encircled by the life line. This area is called the mount of Venus. We will be discussing the mounts in the next chapter.

The tip phalange represents willpower and the second phalange relates to logic. As we are looking for balance in palmistry, we want these two phalanges to be roughly equal in length. This gives the person an equal amount of willpower and logic. He or she will think first and will then act.

If the tip section (willpower) is longer than the second phalange (logic), the person will act without thinking the matter through. People with this formation make many mistakes as they go through life, but pick themselves up again each time, and keep on going. Often, they become extremely successful, since they do not know when to stop.

It is much more common to find people with a second (logic) phalange that is longer than the first. These people

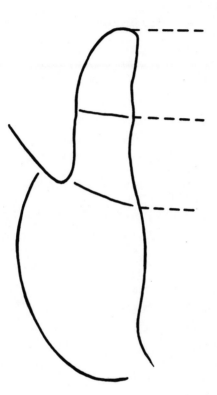

Figure 40: The Three Phalanges of the Thumb

get plenty of ideas, but never quite get around to acting on them. They procrastinate and dream about all the great things they are going to do one day.

The tips of the thumb follow the system of hand shapes that d'Arpentigny devised one hundred and fifty years ago.

If the tip of the thumb is square in shape, the person will be down-to-earth, practical, capable, and have a strong sense of what is right and wrong.

If the tip is spatulate, the person will have an inventive mind and an inquisitive nature. He or she will always keep busy.

If the tip is conic, the person will be graceful, charming, and refined. A conic tip often belongs to a thumb that has a "waisted" second phalange. This means that the second phalange curves inwards on both sides and appears to have a waist. People with a waisted second phalange are diplomatic, caring, and tactful. If you know someone who can say "no" in such a gentle way that you are halfway down the street before you realize what he or she has said, you will know someone with a waisted second phalange.

If the tip appears to taper towards the end, the person will be a deep thinker, who can convey bad news in a gentle, caring manner.

If the tip is flat and broad, the person will be methodical and careful, deliberating at length before acting.

You will also occasionally come across what is known as the "murderer's thumb." The first phalange of this type of thumb appears to be a knob resting on top of the second phalange (figure 41). It indicates that the person will be tolerant and patient for a long while, but then something

Figure 41: Murderer's Thumb

trivial will cause them to erupt in anger. This is probably the reason why this thumb gained its bad name. In fact, this type of thumb is usually inherited. Many years ago I read the palm of a man with "murderer's thumbs," and he told me that his father, grandfather, and infant son all had identical thumbs.

You will now understand that palmistry is much more than the lines on the palm. In the next chapter we are going to take everything a step further by looking at the mounts.

6

The Mounts

The mounts are nine areas on the palm of the hand (figure 42). They are all named after planets, showing the close association palmistry has had with astrology throughout its history. The qualities of the Greek and Roman gods who were named after these planets were also well known to the population, providing a system of keywords for each finger and mount. This became a simple mnemonic system that helped people to learn and understand the meanings of each finger and mount. Many of these keywords are still just as useful today. For instance, the word "mercurial" comes from Mercury, and "saturnine" from Saturn.

The mounts reveal the person's interests and consequently are extremely useful in helping people choose a career that they will be happy in. They also reveal how much energy the person is prepared to put into that particular area of his or her life.

They are called mounts, because they are usually raised protrusions on the palm of the hand. However, this can cause complications, since they are not necessarily raised.

A well-developed, high mount shows that the person has good potential in the area indicated by the mount. Conversely, an underdeveloped, hollow mount shows a lack of promise or potential in that particular area. Most people's mounts are neither high nor low. Consequently, flat mounts should be considered normal.

It can be helpful to regard mounts as banks of energy. A large, high, full mount contains much more energy than a mount that lies flat on the palm. Consequently, large mounts reveal the person's interests and enthusiasms. Naturally, we all pay most attention to activities that we enjoy doing. Consequently, we exert more energy and enthusiasm in these areas than we do on activities that we have to do, but do not necessarily enjoy.

The height and quality of the mounts change to reflect you. (After all, your hand is a map of your mind.) Sometimes these changes occur extremely quickly. You can prove this yourself, by feeling the mounts on your hands at different times. Examine them when you are feeling full of energy, and again when you are feeling tired. You will notice a distinct difference. If you want to gain more of the positive attributes of a specific mount, you need to exercise it. For instance, you can increase the size and quality of your mount of Venus by having sex more frequently. (There are also lines of sexual satisfaction on the mount of Venus. They are found on the side of the palm between the wrist and the start of the second phalange of the thumb.

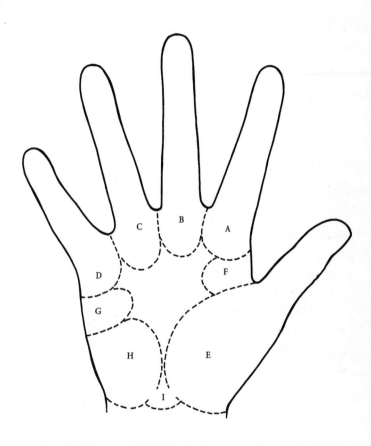

A. Mount of Jupiter   D. Mount of Mercury   G. Mount of Outer Mars
B. Mount of Saturn   E. Mount of Venus   H. Mount of Luna
C. Mount of Apollo   F. Mount of Inner Mars   I. Mount of Neptune

Figure 42: The Mounts

They indicate the degree of pleasure and satisfaction the person is experiencing in his or her love life.)

The most obvious mount, and certainly the easiest to find, is the mount of Venus, which is the area of the palm at the base of the thumb that is encircled by the life line. There is a mount at the base of each finger, also. For instance, the mount of Jupiter is found immediately below the Jupiter finger. Likewise, the mount of Mercury is found at the base of the Mercury finger.

Below the mount of Mercury, halfway down the hand, is the mount of outer Mars, and below this is the mount of Luna.

At the base of the palm, in the center, between the mounts of Luna and Venus is the mount of Neptune.

Finally, between the mounts of Jupiter and Venus is the mount of inner Mars.

Ideally, we want the mounts to be high (raised) and wide. This is because high mounts show that the person is prepared to put energy and enthusiasm into the area that is related to the particular mount. Wide mounts show that the person will put mental effort into that area, as well.

It takes practice to locate and assess the mounts. They are often easier to see if the hand is held at eye level while you look down the palm. The subject is complicated because not every mount will be raised, and some of them are likely to be displaced. For instance, the mount of Mercury is often sited between the Mercury and Apollo fingers, rather than directly under the finger it relates to.

While looking at the mounts, determine which one is the most prominent in the hand. Press on this mount to see how firm it is. A firm mount shows that the person has gained knowledge, which he or she is utilizing. A soft mount reveals that the person has gained knowledge, but is not making good use of it.

Frequently, it is impossible to determine which mount is the dominant one on the hand. All the mounts will appear to be equally well developed. This is a sign of confidence and capability. People with hands like this are ambitious, enthusiastic goal-setters, who aim high and usually achieve their goals. This is why hands like this are known as "lucky hands."

Conversely, you will also come across hands that appear to be lacking in mounts. This is not the case, of course. The mounts are all there, but are simply not developed. People with hands like this are lacking in confidence and have major doubts about their abilities. However, our hands are a map of our potential. Over a period of time, it is possible to change a hand like this with concerted effort. However, someone with a hand that appears to be lacking in mounts will have to work a great deal harder to achieve his or her goals than someone else who has a "lucky hand."

Palmists differ in the amount of attention they pay to the mounts. William Benham, in both of his books, considers the mounts to be the most important single aspect on the palm.[1] Other palmists, including Cheiro, cover the subject in a page or two. I tend to be somewhere between these two extremes. William Benham's books were the greatest single influence on my palmistry career, and I have spent an enormous amount of time researching and studying the mounts. If the mounts virtually leap out to greet me when I first look at someone's hands, I will pay more attention to them than any other part of the hand. If they are not immediately obvious, which is usually the case, I will examine them after assessing the shapes of the hand and the major lines. With most people, I use the mounts to determine the person's interests and to confirm other factors I have seen on the hand.

The Mount of Jupiter

Keywords: jovial (from *Jove*, the Roman form of Jupiter), benevolence, generosity, independence, philosophy, leadership, ambition, confidence, and justice

The mount of Jupiter (A) is found at the base of the first finger. A high, wide mount that is sited directly under the finger reveals someone with intelligence, good self-esteem, and leadership qualities. This gives the person the desire and ambition to achieve his or her goals and to become successful.

You are most likely to find a well-developed mount of Jupiter on the hands of charismatic religious leaders and people in public life. When the mount of Jupiter is strong, all the other mounts on the hand will be, also. I have never seen a strong mount of Jupiter on a hand that also contained weak or negative mounts.

When this mount is deficient, or even flat, the person will suffer from low self-esteem and lack of confidence. He or she will lack ambition and feel awkward in social situations.

If the mount is high, but feels spongy to the touch, the person will be vain and egotistical. He or she will show off, and always want to be the center of attention. This person is also likely to overindulge in anything that interests him or her. Food is one of the most likely areas.

The mounts under the fingers should ideally be found directly below the finger that they relate to. Frequently, though, they are displaced and this alters the interpretation.

If the mount of Jupiter is displaced towards the side of the hand the person will be egotistical. If it is displaced towards the Saturn finger the person will be self-conscious, thoughtful, and interested in learning. Occasionally, it will be found displaced towards the thumb. This means that the person will be extremely aware of his or her family background and heritage, and this will color and influence everything he or she does.

The Mount of Saturn

Keywords: saturnine, traditional values, reliability, responsibility, conscientious, introspective, and solitary

The mount of Saturn (B) is found under the Saturn finger. It is usually the least prominent mount on the hand, which is fortunate, since it is relates to the saturnine qualities. When this mount is well developed, the person will be conscientious and hard-working, but will also be gloomy, melancholy, and solitary. He or she will enjoy work that is involved and detailed, and that can be done with little or no input from others. He or she will find it hard to express love and affection. People with a well-developed mount of Saturn have a strong interest in philosophy, religion, and law. They enjoy research and locating the hidden truths that lie under the surface.

Most people have a flat area under the Saturn finger, and consequently do not have any of the negative qualities that can be created by this mount. These people are independent, and are able to spend time on their own without feeling lonely.

If the mount of Saturn is displaced towards the Jupiter finger, the person will gain optimism and a positive attitude. This is also the case when the mount is displaced towards the Apollo finger. However, these people will still need a large amount of time on their own.

Mount of Apollo

Keywords: enthusiasm, appreciation of beauty, creativity, self-expression, harmony, and people skills

The mount of Apollo (C) is a positive mount that is found at the base of the Apollo, or ring, finger.

A well-developed mount here gives the possessor enthusiasm, people skills, good taste, and a shrewd eye for money-making opportunities. This person will also be adaptable, versatile, and easy to get along with. He or she will enjoy entertaining and being entertained.

If this mount is wide, as well as high, the person will be vain and tend to exaggerate. He or she will have a desire to impress others.

If this mount is soft and spongy, the person will fantasize about all the great things he or she is going to do, but will seldom do anything to achieve them. This person will use charm and enthusiasm to carry people along on his flights of fancy, and they will believe him, at least for a while. He or she will be self-indulgent, vain, and insincere.

Sometimes this mount will appear to be nonexistent. This is a sign that the person lacks imagination, and has little interest in aesthetic pursuits. However, he or she will be extremely practical.

The mount of Apollo is often related to creativity. If this mount is displaced slightly towards the Saturn finger, the person will have a greater interest in creating beautiful things than in performing in public. He or she might, for instance, write plays, rather than perform in them. This placement also means the person will always relate well with young people, and would do well in a career that involved children.

If this mount is slightly displaced towards the Mercury finger, this person will be interested in performing, directing, or producing. He or she will enjoy being in the limelight. Interestingly, this placement also gives the person an affinity with all living things, so he or she may become interested in gardening or keep a number of pets.

Mount of Mercury

Keywords: communication, verbal skills, quick thinking, spontaneous, and mentally alert

The mount of Mercury (D) is sited at the base of the little finger. It relates to clear thinking and self-expression.

People with a well-developed mount of Mercury are interested in the world around them, and enjoy competition and mental challenges. They are affectionate, entertaining, and easy to get along with. They make good partners, parents, and friends. They generally do well in business, since they are shrewd and good judges of character. All of this is accentuated if the little finger is also long.

If both the mounts of Apollo and Mercury are well developed the person will have considerable potential as a public speaker, and be interested in debating and oratory.

If the mount of Mercury is undeveloped, the person is likely to be insincere, deceptive, and full of grandiose, but impractical, schemes. This person is likely to have communication problems inside his or her close relationships.

This mount is frequently displaced towards the mount of Apollo. This gives the person a cheerful, positive, carefree approach towards life. This refusal to take anything seriously can sometimes work to this person's disadvantage. If this mount is displaced towards the side of the hand, the person will display amazing courage in the face of danger.

Sometimes the Apollo and Mercury mounts appear to be one large, single mount. People with this formation on their hands are highly creative, "idea" people. They can do well in any field that involves creativity and communication, but usually need some direction and guidance from others to avoid scattering their energies in too many directions.

Mount of Venus

Keywords: passion for life, warmth, love, sensuality, vitality, stamina, and love of life

The mount of Venus (E) is found at the base of the thumb and is bounded by the life line. This mount relates to love, affection, passion, and vitality.

If this mount is reasonably high the person will be positive, enthusiastic, loving, and sympathetic. He or she will thoroughly enjoy life and be happiest inside the right relationship. He or she will be passionate about life and have plenty of energy and enthusiasm.

This mount is an important factor in determining compatibility. The height of the mount reveals how passionate the person is. Obviously, a relationship where one person has a high mount of Venus, but the other has an almost flat mount, would have enormous problems. In practice, we want the heights of the two mounts of Venus to be about the same.

The life line determines how wide this mount is. A large mount of Venus reveals someone who is generous, giving, understanding, and considerate. He or she will also be open-minded, warm, and enthusiastic.

A narrow mount of Venus, created when the life line hugs the thumb, reveals someone who is cautious, listless, and lacking in energy and passion.

Mount of Mars

Keywords: courage, decisiveness, and persistence

There are two mounts of Mars, known as the inner and outer Mars. Inner Mars (F), sometimes known as positive Mars, is found inside the life line, between the Jupiter finger and the thumb. It is the small piece of flesh that folds when the thumb is moved.

The mount of inner Mars reveals whether or not the person can stand up for himself or herself. It relates to aggression, and also shows how physically courageous the person is. This mount should be firm to the touch. People with strong mounts of inner Mars often go into careers where these qualities can be utilized. The police and the armed forces are two examples. If this mount is soft and spongy, the person will be lacking in confidence and unable to stand up for himself or herself.

Directly across the palm from this mount lies the mount of outer Mars (G), sometimes known as negative Mars, which is usually situated between the head and heart lines. Sometimes the head line will finish on this mount, but the heart line is always below it. The mount of outer Mars relates to self-control and moral courage. When this mount is firm to the touch, the person is able to withstand everything that life sends his or her way, and to keep on going long after everyone else has given up.

If one of these mounts is strong, the chances are that the other one will be, also. However, as long as one of the mounts is firm, the person will stick up for his or her friends, and anything else that is strongly believed in.

Strong mounts of Mars are essential for success in any competitive field, such as sports. This is because this mount gives the person sufficient energy, determination, aggression, persistence, and a strong desire to win.

The area in the center of the palm between these two mounts is known as the plain of Mars. Like the mounts, it should be firm to the touch. A good way to test this is to place your fingers on the back of the person's hand while applying pressure with your thumb on the other side.

When the plain of Mars is firm all the lines that cross it (destiny, head, and heart) can be used to the utmost. When the plain of Mars is weak or spongy the person will be easily influenced by others and make major mistakes in choosing friends. Many teenagers have a weak plain of Mars, but, fortunately, it usually firms as they mature.

Mount of Luna

Keywords: sensitivity, emotions, subconscious, creativity, imagination, intuition, and travel

The mount of Luna (H) is situated across the palm from the thumb, at the base of the hand on the little finger side. It relates to the person's emotional nature, and also governs his or her imagination and creativity. It is also related to mysticism, spirituality, and intuition.

Like the others, this mount should be firm to the touch. It should also have a clear apex. This is a skin ridge pattern, similar to the fingerprints. This denotes a strong, creative imagination. However, if this is the main mount on the hand, the person will be inclined to daydream and be lacking in the necessary push and persistence to achieve his or her dreams. If this is the dominant mount on a man's hand, he is likely to be effeminate. If it is the dominant mount on a woman's hand, she is likely to be frivolous, scattered, and superficial.

If the mount of Luna is high, the person will have a strong interest in travel.

If this mount is deficient or lacking, the person will deal only in concrete facts and have no interest in fantasy or the imagination.

Mount of Neptune

Keywords: speaking skills, quickness of the mind, and connection between the conscious and subconscious

The mount of Neptune (I) is found at the base of the hand, next to the wrist, and joining the mounts of Venus and Luna. When it is firm it creates a level surface at the base of the hand where all three mounts meet.

A well-developed mount of Neptune gives the person the ability to speak in public and to think quickly on his or her feet. Not surprisingly, it is usually found on the hands of entertainers and anyone else who has to speak in public.

This mount connects Venus with Luna, which symbolize our conscious and subconscious energies. If it is equal in height to Venus and Luna the person can come up with good ideas and then make them happen.

7

The Quadrangle

The quadrangle is the name given to the part of the hand that lies between the heart and head lines. For most people these lines are between half an inch and an inch apart for most of their length, widening at each end (figure 43). Naturally, with larger hands the gap is correspondingly greater.

The quadrangle should be firm to the touch and not be overly deep. The deeper this area is, the more introspective and inward-looking the person will be.

People who have average quadrangles are easy to get along with, and are well balanced and stable. They are prepared to help others when necessary, and have a good sense of humor. They also have a good balance between emotion and logic, especially if both the heart and head lines curve towards the end.

If the head and heart lines are close together for much of their length the person will be lacking in imagination. He or she will also tend to be miserly, narrow-minded, and lacking in humor. There is usually a degree of nervous tension present when the quadrangle is too narrow.

When the head and heart lines are well apart the person will be independent, sociable, and easy to get along with. However, he or she is also likely to be gullible, easily led, and overly keen to please. The further apart the head and heart lines are, the more unconventional, outgoing, and extroverted the person will be.

The space between the heart and head lines determines how generous the person will be. A narrow space reveals someone with miserly characteristics, whereas a large space reveals someone who is generous in every way, not just with money.

Sometimes the quadrangle has a "waisted" formation where the ends are much wider than the middle. The area inside the quadrangle denotes the years thirty-five to forty-nine. When the quadrangle is "waisted" the person will feel restless, unsettled, and lack confidence during that time period.

Often, the quadrangle is irregular in shape, being much wider at one end than the other. People who have this formation are likely to be on top of the world at one moment, and then down in the depths a short time later.

If the quadrangle is wider at the percussion side (little finger side) of the palm than it is at the other end, the person will be sensitive, reasonable, and easy to get on with.

If the quadrangle is narrower at the percussion side than the other, the person will find it hard to express his or her feelings out loud. This person is also likely to be stubborn and rigid in outlook.

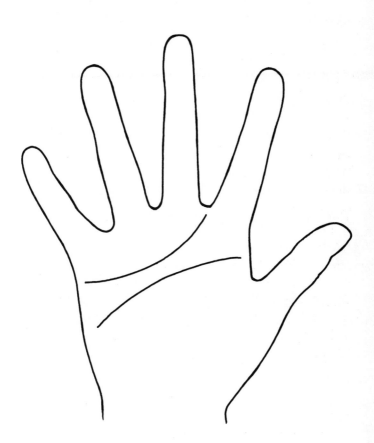

Figure 43: The Quadrangle

Lines Inside the Quadrangle

Ideally, we do not want any lines inside the quadrangle, except for those, such as the destiny line, which always pass through the quadrangle. The hepatica (health line) is another example. Other lines tend to impede the person's progress and cause confusion and worry. A total absence of lines in the quadrangle is not good, either. It indicates that the person is not growing and maturing inwardly as he or she progresses through life. Marks, such as a cross, star, or square, are usually a good sign when found inside the quadrangle. (We will be discussing these marks in the next chapter.)

The period marked out by the quadrangle (ages thirty-five to forty-nine) is an important one. The person is still young, but has developed maturity and is likely to be reassessing his or her progress up to this point, before moving on. Many people experience a complete change of direction while they are in this stage. This is most likely to be a change of career or of partner, but the changes can be in any area of the person's life.

In this stage the person is reaping the benefits of everything that he or she has done up until this moment. If nothing has been achieved yet, this is likely to be a sobering time when the person realizes that all the dreams of his or her youth will never happen unless he or she starts moving ahead quickly.

It is common for people who have achieved nothing to virtually give up at this stage, and spend the rest of their lives blaming others for their lack of success. These people will have a destiny line that ends inside the quadrangle.

Fortunately, we all have the power and ability to change. I have seen a number of cases where the destiny line began to lengthen when the person realized that sitting back and moaning was not going to work, and if they wanted to progress they had to start. Once people become aware of and start acting on the old adage, "if it's going to be, it's up to me," their destiny lines will grow to reflect this change in outlook.

People who have already achieved a degree of success are likely to use this time to expand and progress further. In these cases the destiny line is likely to extend well beyond the heart line.

Occasionally, you will see a destiny line that breaks down into a series of small lines or dots inside the quadrangle. This is a sign of total failure, so much so that the person lacks the desire or strength to try to become successful again. This is a tragedy, but again I have seen examples where people with this have finally taken control of their life again, and created a destiny line that again moved forward. It is in instances like this where a sensitive and caring palm reader can help enormously, and guide and motivate the person to start again.

It is common to see a large cross inside the quadrangle. One side of the cross is formed by the destiny line, and another line crosses this diagonally. This is a sign of ultimate success, but after a great deal of difficulty and many setbacks. Whenever I see it on a hand I always encourage the person to be persistent, because this cross can be extremely frustrating, even for normally patient people.

Every now and again you will find another cross inside the quadrangle, formed by two minor lines. This is known as the mystic cross and people with it have a strong interest in the psychic world.

The Great Triangle

The great triangle is formed by three major lines. Two sides are formed by the life and head lines. The third line is usually formed by the destiny line, but it can also be the hepatica (health) line.

Naturally, most people have a great triangle on their hands. If it is even and well formed, the person will be gracious, broad-minded, and sympathetic. We want this triangle to be as large as possible. A small triangle is related to narrow-mindedness and selfishness.

The triangle should be easy to find on the hand. It is a sign of weakness of character when the great triangle is faint or badly defined.

In Indian palmistry it is believed that if all three corners of the triangle are closed the person will be good at saving money.

If the angle created by the head and life lines is closed and well formed, the person will be refined and have good taste. This is also a sign of caution, as you already know. If the degree of the angle is large, the person will lack aesthetic sense, and be coarse and unrefined. Also, if the angle is open, rather than closed, the person will be independent and impulsive.

The angle formed by the head and destiny lines should be large. This denotes good health and a quick brain.

If the lines of life and destiny are joined at the start of the great triangle it denotes a dependent nature. The further apart they are at the start, the more generous and independent the person will be.

The most important aspect of the great triangle is that it reveals when the person is about to achieve great success. If someone has been working hard in his career for many years, and then suddenly makes a breakthrough and becomes famous, you can be sure that the breakthrough will have been visible in his palm for a short time before it occurred.

If you glance at a hand and immediately notice the great triangle, you can be certain that great success is imminent. Sometimes the great triangle is so noticeable that it appears to virtually jump out of the palm.

8

Marks on the Hand

Most of the finer lines and markings on the hand are caused by stress, tension, and worry. This is why high-strung people appear to have thousands on lines on their hands, while their more placid friends may have just a few.

However, there are a number of marks on the hand that can be identified and interpreted. These include squares, grilles, crosses, stars, and circles (figure 44). By far the most important of these are the squares.

Remember that minor markings can appear and disappear quickly. If you are experiencing a time of uncertainty and feel that you are unable to handle the situation, you may find a few stars appearing in your hands. However, as soon as your life is on an even keel again, the stars will fade away and gradually disappear.

Squares

There are two types of squares. Protective squares, as their name implies, help to protect and nurture the person.

Other squares indicate restrictions and limitations. We can find both of these types on the life line.

A protective square is one that encloses a break in any line. It is most commonly found protecting a break in the life line. It is a fortunate sign, indicating that the person will have enough energy and strength of character to handle a potentially dangerous situation. On the life line, if the square had not been present, the person may have become seriously ill. On other lines, it is an indication that the person will ultimately overcome whatever difficulties are indicated by the line.

A square on the life line that does not cover a break is an example of a restrictive square. This is a sign of confinement. It usually means a term of imprisonment, of course, although I have seen a few examples of people with it who felt themselves completely trapped in a situation and had not known how to get out of it. In this case, other indications on the hand will reveal the reasons why the person felt trapped and confined.

Fortunately, squares of confinement can be removed by changing one's way of life.

A square on the mount of Venus that is not attached to the life line indicates a period of emotional confinement. A lady I read for some years ago had several of these on her palm. She was a codependent person who had a history of being abused by every one of her partners. This was revealed by a chained heart line, as well as the squares on her mount of Venus.

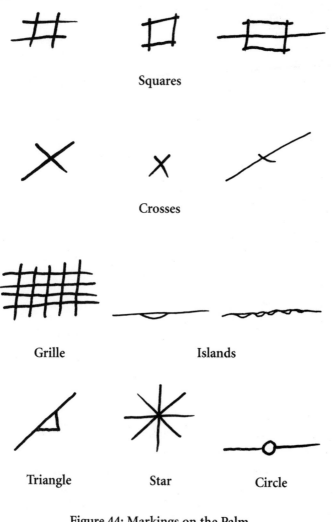

Squares

Crosses

Grille   Islands

Triangle   Star   Circle

Figure 44: Markings on the Palm

Teacher's Square

The teacher's square is a square created by four minor lines either on, or just below, the mount of Jupiter. It is a sign that the person is able to impart knowledge in such a way that other people can easily understand it. People who have this square make natural teachers, and can explain things clearly to others. Consequently, it is found on the hands of the very best teachers. However, many teachers do not have this indication on their hands. People who simply drift into teaching are unlikely to have this square on their hands.

In fact, you are quite likely to find a teacher's square on the hands of people who have no desire to teach at all. These people would have made excellent teachers, and this talent will come out in various ways. Often, at some stage of their lives, these people will use this skill, perhaps by conducting workshops or classes on a hobby or interest that appeals to them.

Most of us can recall a special teacher who helped us enormously. This teacher would certainly have had a teacher's square on his or her hand.

Grilles

Grilles are created by several minor lines, creating a crisscross pattern of lines that looks like a grill. They are usually found on the mounts. These are invariably negative, and indicate that the person wastes a great deal of time and energy, because he or she has not thought something through before acting. This can be extremely frustrating to the individual, since often he or she can not see the situation clearly.

If a grille is situated where a mount should be, but the mount is flat and invisible, it is considered a sign of a cold emotional nature. On a normal size mount, the grille represses the positive qualities of the mount and often enhances the negative qualities.

On the mount of Venus, a grille accentuates the natural passion of the individual. It also relates to a lack of control.

On the mount of Luna it creates a restless, scattered imagination. People with a grille here are usually discontented and hard to please.

On the mount of Jupiter it is inclined to make the person selfish, snobbish, and proud.

On the mount of Saturn it emphasizes the natural saturnine gloominess. It gives the person a morbid approach to life.

On the mount of Apollo it increases the desire for fame, but also encourages the person to scatter his or her energies. People with this grille are often vain, conceited, and inclined to show off.

On the mount of Mercury it shows that the person will not hesitate to stretch the truth when it suits him or her. People with this grille are frequently dishonest in small ways.

Crosses

You will sometimes find a minor line crossing a major line, creating a small cross on the palm. This is a sign of change. You will have to examine the major line carefully to determine if the change is positive or negative. The cross needs to be distinct to be interpreted. A negative cross relates to disappointments and setbacks.

Other crosses can be formed by two minor lines. These need to be easily visible to be interpreted. This is because people with a nervous disposition have hands with many fine lines, most of which are ignored in an interpretation.

Crosses formed by two minor lines are, with just two exceptions, negative, and can be considered warning signs. A cross touching the destiny line indicates the potential for an accident. A cross touching the life line indicates the likelihood of home and family difficulties. A cross touching the hepatica is an indication of an impending illness.

As these crosses are warnings, the problem indicated can be averted by taking the correct action. For instance, if you have a cross touching your hepatica, you should pay attention to your physical well-being. It would pay to have a medical checkup. You might want to look at your diet and the amount of exercise you do. By taking precautionary action in these ways, the cross will disappear.

There are two positive types of cross on the hand. A cross inside the quadrangle, that is created by the destiny line and a minor line, is a sign of ultimate success. However, it is achieved after much hard work and difficulty. Consequently, although it is a positive marking, it can also be an extremely frustrating one, since everything seems to take forever to achieve.

A cross on the mount of Jupiter, created by two minor lines, is a sign that the person is ready to move ahead in a new direction. This frequently involves a new partner, but it is also related to self-awareness and spiritual growth.

A cross on the other mounts is a sign of a major obstacle that needs to be overcome. A cross on the mount of Mercury, for instance, indicates that the person will have great difficulty in expressing himself or herself.

Islands

Islands are small ovals inside a major line. A series of them create an effect like braiding along the line. They are most commonly found on the heart line and relate to emotional ups and downs. On the life line, islands indicate periods of illness. On other lines they relate to uncertainty, frustration, and an unwillingness to move forward.

Triangles

Small triangles on the palm are found occasionally and show that the person has a shrewd brain and can quickly understand the essentials of a situation. They are usually found on the mounts, and increase the quality of the mount they are on. A triangle is always a positive sign and is often an indication that the person will find success in a creative or scientific career. Interestingly, a triangle on the mount of Venus is a sign that the person will marry for money, and that the relationship will be a success. A triangle gives the owner enormous mental clarity in the field indicated by the mount.

Stars

A star is created by four or five minor lines crossing each other to create a star-like marking on the hand. It is a positive sign when found on one of the mounts, but is considered negative anywhere else. When found on a mount it is an indication that the person could achieve great success in the field indicated by the particular mount. The best place to find a star is on the mount of Jupiter. This means that the person will be recognized and honored for his or her achievements.

In other parts of the hand a star is an indication of a situation that the person is unable to handle or control.

Circle

It is extremely rare to find a perfect circle on the palm of the hand. On most parts of the hand it is considered a sign of weakness. However, when it is found on the mount of Apollo it is considered to be an indication of great success and even fame.

Dots and Spots

Dots and spots on any of the major lines indicate a blockage of energy. They need to be indented into the palm to be interpreted.

On the life line a dot or spot is likely to be a physical illness. On the heart line, it indicates emotional trauma. (The sole exception to this is a white dot on the heart line. This is a sign of a strong, loving relationship achieved after great difficulty.)

On the head line a dot or spot indicates a period of negativity, with the potential of a breakdown.

On the destiny line a dot or spot indicates a period when the person reviewed his career up to that point.

None of these marks should be interpreted on their own. You always need to confirm your findings by looking at other parts of the hand.

9

Skin Ridge Patterns

A close examination of the surface of the palm shows that in addition to the lines and marks on the hand, the entire surface is made up of extremely fine skin ridge patterns that doctors call epidermal ridges. You will probably need a magnifying glass to examine these.

By far the best-known skin ridge patterns are our fingerprints. The Chinese were the first to recognize the uniqueness of these and used them for identification purposes hundreds of years ago. In 1880, Dr. Henry Faulds, a British doctor, discovered that the ridge patterns on our fingers and thumb could be used to positively identify someone. In 1892, Sir Francis Galton proved that no two fingerprints were the same. Since then, fingerprints have become the major method of identifying criminals all around the world.

In 1926, Dr. Harold Cummins discovered that certain types of fingerprints and epidermal ridges were found in 70 percent of all known Down's syndrome cases.[1] Doctor

Cummins also came up with the term "dermatoglyphics" to describe the fine skin ridge patterns. Doctor Cummins, with Charles Midlo, wrote *Fingerprints, Palms and Soles*, which was published in 1943.[2] Cummins' study created a whole new field of diagnostic medicine which is playing an increasingly important part in everyone's life.

Our fingerprints come in three main variations: loops, whorls, and arches (figure 45). Of these, the loops are by far the most commonly found all around the world.

Loops

People with loops in the fingerprint patterns are able to adjust and fit in to most situations. They are adaptable, versatile, and work well with others. However, they sometimes have trouble in keeping their feelings under control, and can scatter their energies over too wide an area. They also get bored easily, and need variety in their lives to be happy.

A loop on the Jupiter finger makes the person graceful, charming, adaptable, and highly versatile. He or she will be thoughtful and caring.

A loop on the Saturn finger indicates someone with no fixed ideas on anything. This person will enjoy topics that can be considered and discussed, but will change his or her mind freely depending on the audience.

A loop on the Apollo finger enhances the appreciation of beautiful things. This person likes to be at the forefront of any new craze, and is always trying to push back the boundaries.

A loop on the Mercury finger indicates someone who can learn quickly and easily. He or she will have considerable

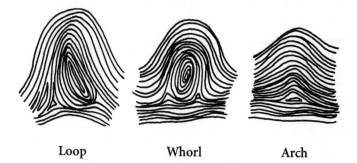

Loop   Whorl   Arch

Figure 45: Three Main Types of Fingerprint Patterns

verbal skills and will have a knack for saying the right thing at the right time.

A loop on the thumb makes the person diplomatic and tactful, even while being strongly stubborn. Consequently, this person will usually get his or her own way.

Whorls

People with whorls (concentric circles) in their fingerprints are independent and individualistic in outlook. Whorls give originality to whatever quality the finger represents. Blessed with ambition and persistence, people with a whorl on their hands are self-motivated and often become extremely successful. They enjoy analyzing situations and do not like to be hurried into making decisions. People with more than one whorl on their hands are frequently secretive and suspicious of the motives of others. It is extremely rare to meet anyone with whorls on every finger.

A whorl on the Jupiter finger makes the person ambitious and determined to succeed. This person will capitalize on his original and unorthodox ideas and may become extremely successful. This person needs to find his or her own way, and sometimes has difficulty in finding exactly the right niche in life.

A whorl on the Saturn finger makes the person analytical. He or she enjoys the details of things and is not easily swayed by the ideas or opinions of others.

A whorl on the Apollo finger reveals a highly original, creative person with a distinctly unusual approach. Although this person will deliberately set out to shock others at times, he or she will inwardly hold conservative views that have been learned through experience. Whorls are most commonly found on the Apollo finger.

A whorl on the Mercury finger creates an excellent conversationalist with original ideas. He or she will have distinct interests and will have no desire to explore other topics.

A whorl on the thumb makes the person determined, stubborn, and highly ambitious. This person is prepared to work as long as is necessary to achieve his or her goals.

Arches

People with arches in their fingerprint patterns are conscientious, stable, cautious, and reliable. They are practical people who are prepared to work hard and long, when necessary. They are reserved and serious in outlook. They are also persistent and like to get their own way.

An arch on the Jupiter finger indicates someone who enjoys power for its own sake, and will persevere for as long as is necessary to achieve it. When found on both first fingers, arches make it hard for the person to discuss his or her innermost feelings.

An arch on the Saturn finger reveals that the person does not like to talk about himself or herself. This reticence is especially strong when discussing ambitions or personal philosophy.

An arch on the Apollo finger in unusual. It inhibits the natural sense of beauty associated with Apollo, but enhances the practical skills of designing and making something useful. Someone with this combination may, for instance, become a potter rather than a painter because pottery can often be useful as well as attractive. These people often have mechanical or scientific interests.

An arch on the Mercury finger inhibits the verbal skills emphasized by Mercury. Consequently, these people are often quiet and secretive, especially when their career is involved.

An arch on the thumb gives the person a sensible, practical, and often dull approach to life. He or she is likely to be suspicious of the motives of others.

Tented Arches

If the arch is high, it is called a "tented arch." People with these are high-strung and nervous. They are impulsive, enthusiastic, and often creative, usually in a musical field. They are inclined to overreact in times of crisis.

A tented arch on the Jupiter finger often gives the bearer a charmed life. The person will achieve his or her goals, and have a great deal of fun in the process, surrounded by a loving family and friends.

A tented arch on the Saturn finger makes the person serious and idealistic. This person is likely to spend a great deal of time in a world of his or her own, in preference to dealing with the everyday problems of life.

A tented arch on the Apollo finger makes the person an enthusiastic, emotional, impulsive, daydreamer, full of impractical ideas and schemes. This person is likely to be artistic, but needs careful guidance by others to achieve his or her potential.

A tented arch on the Mercury finger is rare, and gives the person considerable skills at speaking and writing. This person is likely to be a humanitarian, and use his or her talents for the benefit of others.

A tented arch on the thumb enables the person to fit in to any type of situation and get along well others. This person is naturally diplomatic, and achieves his or her goals with gentle persuasion and charm.

Tri-Radii

The tri-radii (sometimes known as apexes) are small triangles created by the skin ridge pattern (figure 46). They frequently look like a three-pointed star. Most people have between four and six of these on their palms. The easiest ones to find are located below the fingers on the mounts. Other tri-radii can be found on the mount of Luna, and occasionally on the mount of Neptune. A tri-radius here is a sign that the person has a strong psychic potential.

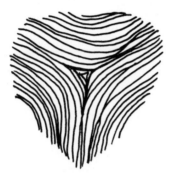

Figure 46: Tri-Radius

The tri-radii on the finger mounts should ideally be sited at the top of each mount. After all, another name for tri-radius is apex, which means at the top. When found in this position they enhance the potential of the particular mount. However, the tri-radii are more frequently found further down the mount, or even beside it.

Beryl Hutchinson suggests that we consider the mounts to be power houses of energy, and regard the tri-radii as switches that turn on and direct the energy.[3] Consequently, the tri-radius is the apex, or central position of the mount, regardless of where it is actually located.

Apex of Jupiter

Ideally, the tri-radius on the mount of Jupiter is centrally sited on the mount, and exactly in line with the center of the finger. Someone with this siting will be honest, ethical, trustworthy, and a person of honor and integrity.

It is far more likely that the tri-radius will be sited towards the Saturn finger. In this position, the basic interpretation of the mount of Jupiter still applies, but is put towards a more practical application.

When the tri-radius is close to the thumb side of the palm, the person lacks a sense of responsibility and will take unnecessary chances that may or may not work.

If the tri-radius is located close to the base of the Jupiter finger the person will have an intellectual approach to the world. He or she may appear condescending and supercilious to others.

If the tri-radius is centrally sited but well away from the base of the Jupiter finger, the person will utilize his personal faith or philosophy to help others.

Apex of Saturn

When the tri-radius is situated directly below the Saturn finger, the person will be straightforward, direct, and possess good judgment.

If it is displaced towards the Apollo finger the person will have no sense of the value of money. He or she may be extravagant, squander money, or make unwise investments.

It is extremely rare for the apex of Saturn to be displaced toward the Jupiter finger. In fact, I do not recall ever having seen an example of this.

If the tri-radius is located close to the base of the Saturn finger the person will need a great deal of room around him. He or she will be interested in learning, and will be more interested in theories than in practical application.

If the tri-radius is located well away from the base of the Saturn finger the person will have an interest in real estate. This person might well become a real estate investor, broker, or simply show an interest in the subject.

Apex of Apollo

A centrally sited apex gives the person a keen awareness of beauty, along with significant potential in this field. This is accentuated if the apex is close to the base of the Apollo finger.

If the tri-radius is displaced toward the Saturn finger the person will tend to doubt his or her creative abilities. (This placement is almost always found in combination with an Apollo finger that curves toward the Saturn finger.)

If the tri-radius is displaced toward the Mercury finger the person will have the ability to make money out of some form of creativity. This is likely to be work that the person creates himself or herself. However, this person could also become a successful dealer of other people's work.

Apex of Mercury

It is unusual for the apex of Mercury to be centrally sited under the Mercury finger. When found in this position, it gives the person a great love of words, both written and spoken.

This apex is normally displaced toward the Apollo finger. The person's verbal skills lessen the closer this apex is to the Apollo finger.

Loop Patterns

There are thirteen different loops, created by the skin ridge patterns, that can be found on the palm of the hand (figure 47). Most people have one or two loops on their hands. However, since not everyone has them, do not become alarmed if you can not find any in your own palms.

The whole subject of dermatoglyphics is comparatively new in palmistry. I find it fascinating, since original research can still be done in this field.

The Loop of Humor

The loop of humor (A) is found between the Mercury and Apollo fingers. It is the most frequently found of the thirteen loops. It gives the owner a slightly unusual, and decidedly "different," sense of humor. The larger this loop is, the greater the sense of humor. Most people have a sense of humor, and the absence of this loop does not mean that the person is lacking in humor. Someone with it, though, always has a slightly offbeat, wacky sense of humor.

The Loop of Ego

The loop of ego (B) also starts between the Mercury and Apollo fingers, and consequently can occasionally be mistaken for the loop of humor. However, it always slants across and on to the mount of Apollo. It is sometimes known as the "loop of vanity." People with this loop are always aware of their own self-importance and are extremely sensitive at the same time. Consequently, they have vulnerable egos that can be easily hurt.

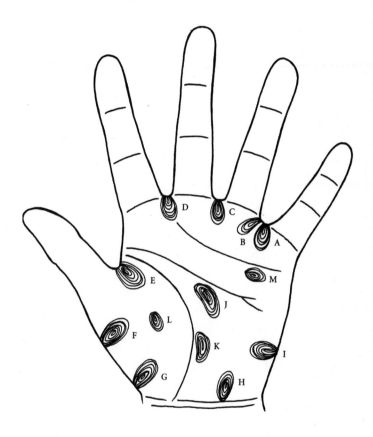

A. Loop of Humor
B. Loop of Ego
C. Loop of Common Sense
D. Rajah Loop
E. Loop of Courage

F. Loop of Response
G. Loop of Music
H. Loop of Inspiration
I. Ulnar Loop
J. Loop of Memory

K. Humanitarian Loop
L. Loop of Stringed Music
M. Loop of Recall

Figure 47: Loop Patterns

The Loop of Common Sense

The loop of common sense (C) is situated between the Apollo and Saturn fingers. People with it think before acting, and seldom do anything impulsive. They also have a strong sense of responsibility and enjoy helping others. Consequently, this loop is also known as the "loop of good intent." People with this loop enjoy being busy and do not like to waste time.

The Rajah Loop

The rajah loop (D) is found between the Saturn and Jupiter fingers. People with it possess a special charisma and inner glow that draws people to them. They are usually successful in their careers and gravitate towards a position of prestige and honor. In traditional Indian palmistry it is believed that people with a rajah loop are descended from royalty.

The Loop of Courage

The loop of courage (E) is on the mount of Mars between the base of the thumb and the start of the life line. People with it are naturally courageous, and show no fear, even in the presence of great danger. They are prepared to stand up and support to the bitter end anything that they believe in.

People with a loop of courage also enjoy hearing about the courageous feats of others, and try to live up to these examples in their own lives. In effect, this loop enhances the positive aspects of the mount of Mars.

The Loop of Response

The loop of response (F) is located on the mount of Venus between the base of the thumb and the wrist. People with this marking are extraordinarily empathetic, and respond instantly to the feelings of the group they happen to be in at the time. If everyone is feeling sad, they will also be sad. If everyone is having a good time, so will they.

They need bright cheerful surroundings because they also respond instantly to their environment. If their surroundings are dull, dirty, and dark, they will immediately feel downhearted and depressed. If the surroundings are cheerful, they will be, too. This response is automatic and instant. If someone with this mark was confined to prison, for example, they would immediately suffer from depression and might even try to kill themselves.

People with this loop should cultivate positive-minded friends and avoid negative people as much as possible.

The loop of response also gives the person a strong liking for brass band music.

The Loop of Music

The loop of music (G) starts at the wrist and lies on the base of the mount of Venus. People with this have a great love of music. It gives a definite talent in this area, and people with it have great potential in the music world as players, composers, or singers. Even if this talent is not developed, the love of music will be strongly evident and will be of great importance in the person's life.

The Loop of Inspiration

The loop of inspiration (H) is found at the base of the hand on the mount of Neptune, between the Venus and Luna mounts. People with this loop are inspired by anything that affects them greatly. This may be a stirring piece of music, a moving book, or a humanitarian or kindhearted deed. People with this loop usually have a strong faith. This is not usually a typical, orthodox faith, but a strong faith or philosophy that they have developed themselves.

People with the loop of inspiration are also highly intuitive and possess a strong, creative imagination.

The loop of inspiration is extremely rare, and people with it have the potential to make the world a better place. The presence of this loop can turn an average musician into a great composer. It is often considered a sign of greatness.

The Ulnar Loop

The ulnar loop (I) is found rising from the side of the palm on the mount of Luna. Only if it is at least halfway along this mount towards the wrist can the person use it to gain access to his or her creative subconscious mind. It invariably means that people with it are motivated more by their subconscious minds, rather than their conscious minds. They often have a rather unusual way of looking at things, which marks them out as being slightly "different."

This loop is found on the palms of at least 90 percent of people suffering from Down's syndrome. It is found on only 8 percent of normal hands.

The ulnar loop is often known as the "loop of nature" since people with it have an intuitive response to the workings of nature. A good dowser or gifted gardener are likely to have this loop on their hands. It is interesting to note that many Down's syndrome people have a great love of nature.

The Loop of Memory

The loop of memory (J) is found in the center of the palm. It runs diagonally across the palm, with one end indicating the mount of Jupiter and the other pointing towards the mount of Luna. It frequently parallels the head line.

People with a loop of memory always have an extremely good memory. The longer this loop is, the more detailed the memory. An acquaintance of mine can instantly name the day and date of anything that has ever happened to him during his life. He has a pronounced loop of memory on both palms.

People with a loop of memory are good at keeping in contact with people from their past, and are able to make good use of these contacts when necessary.

The Humanitarian Loop

The humanitarian loop (K) is extremely rare. It is found near the center of the palm, running parallel to the destiny line and pointing towards the wrist.

People with a humanitarian loop on their hands are idealistic and dream of a perfect world. Because they try to improve the world they live in, they experience a large number of setbacks and disappointments. When found on a strong hand, the humanitarian loop can be an asset, and this person will use his or her considerable abilities to try to make changes that benefit everyone. On a weaker hand, though, the person is likely to become cynical and bitter, and find it hard to live in a less-than-perfect world.

The Loop of Stringed Music

The loop of stringed music (L) is a small, oval loop in the center of the mount of Venus. It, like the loop of music, gives the person a strong interest in music, but in this case the person will have a strong liking for the music of stringed instruments. It is extremely rare.

The Loop of Recall

The loop of recall (M) is a small loop in the quadrangle, usually located between the Mercury and Apollo fingers. People with a loop of recall have amazingly retentive memories and the ability to recall information whenever it is required. The talent is enhanced if the head line runs over this loop.

Scientists and palmists alike are actively researching dermatoglyphics. It is a comparatively new area and the opportunity is still there for original research. Use a magnifying glass to find and classify the various skin ridge markings. Make sure that you take palm prints of clients who have interesting skin ridge patterns. By doing this, you will ultimately have a valuable collection of each possible loop and apex.

Knowledge of the skin ridge patterns can enhance the quality of your readings, but make sure that you fully understand the basics of palmistry before spending too much time exploring the skin ridge patterns.

Remember that the interpretations of the different skin ridge patterns need to be considered in the context of the person's palms. It would be unusual, for instance, to find someone who had both the loop of courage and a weak thumb. However, it is possible, and obviously both factors would need to be considered carefully before giving an evaluation.

10

Health, Wealth, Love, and Happiness

Everyone wants to be healthy, wealthy, deeply in love, and happy. Consequently, as a palmist, you will be asked more questions about these subjects than any other topic. In the next chapter we will do a complete palm reading, and you will see how all of these subjects are incorporated into the reading.

However, many people have specific questions on these topics and you will need to explore them more deeply. The range of questions that can be asked about these three subjects is enormous, but basically boil down to just four questions: *Will I live a long life? Will I be financially secure? Will I have a long-lasting, loving relationship?* and, *Will I be happy?*

Fortunately, it is possible to answer these questions by a close examination of the person's hands.

Health

Our health is our greatest single asset. Consequently, it is not surprising that so many people worry about their health. They are concerned that they may die young, be incapacitated by some illness or accident, or be bedridden and senile in their old age.

Whenever I am asked any question about health, I first determine if the person means physical or emotional health. Obviously, the two are closely connected as the state of our emotional health determines our physical well-being. The person may be under severe pressure and suffering from stress and strain. We can all sustain pressure for a short while, but if it is ongoing, it will ultimately affect our physical health.

The state of our emotional health is revealed in every part of the hand, not just in the number of stress or strain lines. We need to see if the heart line is relatively smooth. Along with this, we need to look at the mount of Venus and the lines of sexual satisfaction. Then we examine the head and destiny lines. If all of these factors appear happy, the person will be enjoying good emotional health.

However, any problems in these areas need to be addressed and corrected before they start affecting the person's physical health.

For physical health, I first look at the hand as a whole. People with broad hands have more energy than people with narrow hands. Consequently, they usually enjoy better health, since they have the energy to overcome minor health problems.

The number of lines on the hands is another clue. Speaking generally, the fewer lines the better from a health point of view. This is because most lines are caused by stress and nervous tension, both factors that can cause ill health.

Only after this will I look at the life line. Ideally, it should be clear, well marked, and reach well across the palm. A large mount of Venus gives vitality and energy, which has an enormous effect on the person's health.

I will look at the number of worry lines. This has a bearing on how the person thinks. Worry lines are only likely to cause health problems if they cross the life line.

Naturally, I also look at the hepatica (health line). Ideally, this line should be absent, since this denotes excellent health. However, if someone is asking questions about his or her health, the chances are high that this line will be present on the palm. Naturally, this line should be clear and free of any islands or breaks.

There is a great deal of research going on today that aims to determine people's predisposition to certain illnesses by examining their palms. In fact, scientists are now confirming many of the things that palmists have known for hundreds, if not thousands, of years.[1]

Always remember that you are a palmist, not a medical practitioner. You must not give medical advice. Be encouraging and supportive when people ask you about their health, and always suggest that they see a medical professional.

Wealth

Money problems are part of life. Charles Dickens' character, Mr. Micawber, expressed the matter very well: "Annual income twenty pounds, annual expenditure nineteen six, result happiness. Annual income twenty pounds, annual expenditure twenty pounds ought and six, result misery."[2]

Since no one ever has enough, you will be asked many questions about this subject.

Money is indicated in three ways on the palm (figure 48). Inherited money is shown by a small line between the third and fourth fingers that curves part of the way around the third finger. Unfortunately, this line is not very helpful. It gives no indication as to when the money will be inherited or how much money is involved. It is simply an indication that the person has, or will, inherit money.

Easy money is shown by a triangle on the inside of the life line. One side of it is made up by the life line, and the other two lines are minor lines. This triangle always indicates a large amount of money.

However, the term "large" depends on what the person considers to be a large amount. A large lotto win, for instance, would be shown as a triangle on the life line. A win of a thousand dollars on a horse race would probably not be shown, because that is not considered a large amount of money these days. However, if you were living on the streets and suddenly won a thousand dollars, that might very well be indicated on the palm, since you would consider that to be a fortune.

Most people have to earn their own money. Their potential is indicated by a small triangle in the center of the hand. Two sides of this are created by the destiny and head lines, and a minor line on the little finger side of the palm creates the third side. This triangle is extremely small and shows the person's potential. It does not necessarily mean that he or she will earn that amount of money over a lifetime.

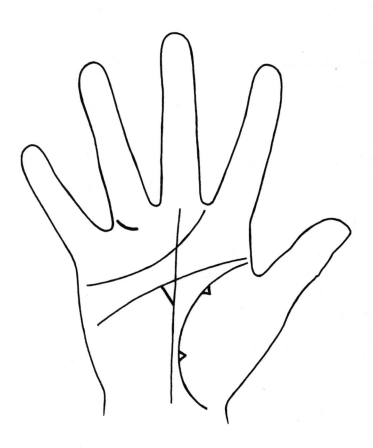

Figure 48: Indications of Money on the Palm

First, we have to see if the person is motivated to achieve it. We determine this by looking at the top two phalanges of the thumb to see if willpower and logic are roughly even. If the second phalange (logic) is much longer than the tip section, the person is probably not going to make much money, since he or she will think, and think, and then think some more. This person is likely to achieve very little.

We also have to look at the head line to see if the person has the necessary brain power to make much money. Remember that a short head line does not mean a lack of intellectual ability. It denotes a quick, sharp, and often highly shrewd thinker. Someone like this could well make a great deal of money, compared to someone with a long head line who enjoys learning for its own sake.

We also need to see if the money triangle is open or closed. If it is closed, the person is able to hang on to some of the money after earning it. If it is open, most of the money will disappear.

A thin line that bisects the minor line (third side of the money triangle) indicates financial difficulties at different times. However, this is not necessarily a bad thing because it can be a spur to progress. This person often takes two steps forward, and then slides back one step. Ultimately, this person may very well be extremely successful, but will be a plodder rather than a "whiz kid."

Sometimes you will see a double money sign. In this case, there are two minor lines that each join the destiny and head lines, creating a small triangle inside a larger one. This is a sign that the person will make money, and will then have investments which create additional money. It is a sign of both earned and unearned income.

I always tell my clients that the amount of money indicated is a potential, and it is up to them to achieve it.

Love

Almost everyone wants to love and be loved in return. It can be exciting to be single and have many different relationships, but sooner or later, most people want to settle down inside a strong, stable, loving, and supportive relationship. People sometimes think that love is only for the young. This is totally wrong. In the course of my career as a palmist I have had people of all ages ask if there would be a "special someone" in their lives.

For questions about love, I look first at the shape of their hand. I then examine the heart line, mount of Venus, and the relationship lines. Finally, I make sure that the thumbs are compatible.

A relationship is much easier if both partners have similarly shaped hands. They will think along similar lines and will tend to agree with each other on most issues. Imagine the potential conflicts that would arise between two people, one with short, stubby fingers and the other with long, graceful fingers.

You can also use the relationship between the four types of hand (fire, earth, air, and water) and the interpretations of what each element means. For instance, fire and water is not usually a good combination, since water puts out fire. However, this is just one factor to look at. I am a Sagittarian (fire) and have been married to my Piscean (water) wife for almost thirty years. However, we both have air-shaped hands and both have physical heart lines ending between the Jupiter and Saturn fingers. Our mounts of Venus are also similar in height and degree of firmness.

The heart line determines the person's emotional life, and you can read the person's ups and downs as he or she progresses through life. A long, clear, and well-marked heart line is an indication of a long, happy, and successful relationship.

Ideally, both people will have heart lines that end in the same place. There will be many difficulties if one person's heart line ends under the Jupiter finger (idealistic) and the other's heart line ends under the Saturn finger (selfish). Naturally, it is also easier if both partners have the same types of heart lines. If both people have a physical heart line, for instance, they will tend to understand each other much more easily than another couple, one of whom has a physical heart line and the other a mental.

The mount of Venus shows how loving and passionate the person is. If this mount is deficient, either by being flat or extremely small, the person will have no need or desire for a vibrant relationship. However, he or she might desire a relationship for companionship.

The relationship lines are only present if the person has important relationships. I have seen married men who have no relationship lines on their hands, but this is rare. The presence of a relationship line that comes up the side of the palm and on to the palmar surface is an indication of an important relationship that lasts for a considerable length of time.

The thumb should also be examined for compatibility. Imagine the potential conflicts between two people who each have incredibly stubborn thumbs. Also, someone with a strong, stubborn thumb would overpower and dominate someone with a small, flexible, giving thumb. This combination might work well for a while, but eventually the person who is being dominated is likely to decide that he or she has had enough, and walk away from the relationship. Almost as difficult is the combination where both people have flexible, giving thumbs. Each would want to please the other, and they would be likely to have problems in making decisions on anything.

Ideally, we want the thumbs to be reasonably similar. The best combinations occur when both partners have strong, but not overly stubborn, thumbs. This means that neither tends to dominate the other, and each will tend to stick up for what really matters to him and her, and will be more flexible in other instances.

These factors all indicate the potential for a relationship. I then look at the heart line to see what the person's future looks like from an emotional point of view. I also look for a fine line running parallel to the heart line at the end to see if the person will, or will not, be lonely in his or her old age.

Every now and again, I will see the hands of a couple wanting to know how compatible they are with each other. I love doing this if they are clearly compatible, but find it much harder when there are major differences in their hands. Obviously, in these instances, I stress the areas of potential disharmony, and how the couple can best handle these areas. The two most important factors for compatibility are the ending positions of the heart lines and the height and firmness of the mount of Venus.

It is better for the relationship if both partners have the same type of heart line (either physical or mental). This is because someone with a mental heart line will constantly need to be told by the other partner that he or she is loved. Someone with a physical heart line will not have that necessity, and will be inclined to underrate the importance of saying words of endearment to his or her partner.

Interestingly, it also pays to check the Mercury fingers as well, when doing a compatibility analysis. A long little finger (reaching past the line dividing the top two phalanges of the ring finger) provides the person with good communication skills. (It is also strongly related to the sex drive—the longer this finger is, the better.) Problems can arise if one person has a long little finger, and is in a relationship with someone with a short Mercury finger. Ideally, we want both partners to have similar-length little fingers.

Happiness

Happiness can be extremely elusive. Most people who come to see me for a palm reading have a problem that they need help with. Consequently, they are unlikely to be happy. However, they have probably had periods of intense happiness in the past, and will have more in the future.

The wisest and most profound advice I have ever been given about happiness was the saying: "If you want to be happy, be happy." It is as simple, and as difficult, as that.

Some people are happy most of the time, no matter what happens to them, and other people seem to enjoy wallowing in misery. It is possible to determine these people, and everything in between, by looking at the person's hands.

For happiness, I look first at the breadth of the hand and the quality of the life line. Both of these are related to the person's energy levels. If the hand is broad and has a well-marked life line that comes well out into the middle of the hand, I know that the person has the potential for great happiness.

I then look at the head line to see if the person is using the intelligence he or she was given at birth. People with questioning, inquiring minds also have the potential for great happiness, because they are always learning and life is a process of discovery.

I also examine the thumb to determine the person's willpower and logic. As you know, in palmistry, we are always looking for balance and want the top two phalanges of the thumb to be roughly equal in length. However, the happiest people usually have a second phalange (logic) that is slightly longer than the first (willpower). People with an abundance of logic enjoy thinking about things. They are not driven or impelled to do things the way someone who has more willpower than logic is. Consequently, they are generally happy.

People who are always nervous and tense are less likely to be happy than people who are calm and placid. Consequently, people with few lines on their hands are generally happier than people who have a network of faint tension lines on theirs.

Finally, I look for the small markings such as squares, triangles, and grilles. These have the potential to upset what would otherwise appear to be a happy hand. Hopefully, the person will have more positive indications than negative. I will have covered the meanings of the different markings in the course of the reading and, if necessary, will suggest which ones should be worked on to create more happiness in the person's life.

I am not asked about happiness very often. Usually, the person will be concerned about the direction of his or her love life, career, or finances. Once the area of concern has been rectified, the person is likely to be content once more. However, contentment is not as strong a feeling as happiness.

Some hands are naturally happy, while others are naturally the opposite. Most people have hands that are somewhere in the middle. Someone with plenty of vitality, an inquiring mind, and few negative markings is likely to be naturally positive and happy. Conversely, someone who is high-strung, with little energy, and a variety of negative markings is equally as likely to be naturally unhappy.

Fortunately, we all have the power to change. This change has to come from within, and takes a great deal of time and effort. However, the rewards can be tremendous.

One of the most satisfying aspects of reading palms is to see how your positive suggestions have been accepted and acted on by your clients, and made visible on their palms.

Success

The degree of success can be measured in the hand. However, the type of success can not. Success means different things to different people. Many people equate it with money, while others relate it to a generally happy life. I consider people to be successful if they are doing what they want to do and are making progress with it. Consequently, according to my definition, a struggling artist may be more successful than a rich and famous film star. If the artist is doing what he or she loves to do, and is learning and growing in the process, that person is successful. The film star might have plenty of money, and appear to be extremely successful. However, he or she might be dysfunctional and desperately unhappy. I would not consider that person to be a success.

A lady I know gave up a promising career in medicine to bring up three children. Some people may believe that she gave up the opportunity for success because of her children. In fact, she considers it to be the other way around. She has done a wonderful job in keeping the family together and in bringing up three happy, well-adjusted children who are now all doing well in their own careers. I consider her to be an extremely successful person.

Another example is a well-known street cleaner in the city I live in. He has swept the streets of the same part of town for some thirty years, and recently published a book about the people he has met in the course of his work. Being a street cleaner is not an obvious choice of career for someone whom I consider to be successful. However, he is an amazing man who takes pride in his work and has become a local celebrity. He also has a happy home and family life.

Any discussion of success is complicated by the fact that someone may have an extremely successful business career, but fail completely in every relationship. I do not consider people to be successful unless they are well rounded and well balanced in their lives. All of this, of course, is easy to see in the hand.

The presence of a destiny line is essential for success. Someone without a destiny line may be lucky every now and again, but will not be working towards a specific goal.

A Sun line is also a major indicator of success. It helps provide the necessary motivation and desire to succeed.

Successful people also have well-developed mounts, and at least one of these will give a clue as to where the person will achieve success.

We have now covered all the essential elements in palmistry. In the next chapter we will put it all together and give someone a palm reading.

11

Putting It All Together

Giving and receiving a palm reading is an intimate experience. When you read someone's palms, you are sitting close to them, holding their hands, and telling them about their character, as well as their past, present, and future. Most people are somewhat nervous when they have their palms read. They do not know what secrets you might see in their palms, and they may be worried that you will predict a painful death or some other disaster.

Consequently, it is important that you make people feel at ease before starting to read their palms. I often spend a few minutes talking about palmistry before asking to see their hands. I stress the fact that their hands can and will change, and that the future is up to them. They have the power to create the sort of future they want for themselves.

I believe that you have a definite duty to stress the positive and to make the people you read for feel better about themselves and their lives. All the same, it is essential that you be honest. Otherwise, there is no point in reading the person's hands in the first place.

I must admit that occasionally I am selectively honest. For instance, what should I say if I am reading the palms of someone who has just married and is extremely happy, but I can see that the marriage is not going to last? Would I be helping this person in any way by telling him or her that? In the course of a quick reading, I would ignore this topic completely, and instead focus on other parts of the hand. I am still being honest with what I say, but I am deliberately holding back certain information.

In practice, I would probably only see such a person while doing quick, fun readings, since most people come to palmists for a full-length reading only when something is going wrong with their lives. If the person came to me because there was a problem with his or her marriage, I would give advice and make suggestions based on what I saw in the person's hands.

You will have to make up your own mind as to how you deal with situations such as this. I believe that quick readings are mainly for fun, and should be upbeat, positive, and encouraging. I might mention one or two negative character traits, but most of the reading will be positive. When giving fun readings it is important to look for good qualities in the hand. If you focus on health, wealth, love, and the person's own interests you will make people happy and your popularity will increase.

Full-length readings are a completely different matter. With these you should be able to discuss everything freely and openly with the client. Usually, the session becomes a conversation where the client opens up and talks about his or her concerns, and the palm reader gives advice based on what is on the client's hands. In many respects a good palm reader is a counselor who can provide a sympathetic ear and good advice.

You need to be gentle with the people you deal with. For years I did palm readings as part of the entertainment for corporate functions. Many of the people who came to me in those situations said that they did not believe in palmistry and were having their palms read simply for the fun of it. I noticed though that even these people listened carefully to what I had to say, and sometimes came back in the course of the evening to ask further questions. Occasionally, I would see these people again years later and find that they had remembered what I had told them virtually word for word.

You will discover exactly the same thing when you start reading palms for people. Consequently, as people will remember and think about what you tell them, the most important rule is to be gentle.

It is better to start out by doing brief readings, the short-er the better. In fact, you can see a large number of palms in a short space of time by simply mentioning your inter-est in the subject everywhere you go. People will not expect to receive a reading in that context and will be thrilled at any comments you may be able to make.

Gradually, as your knowledge and experience grows, you can increase the quality and length of your readings. You can then use your new palmistry skills to help, coun-sel, and advise others.

It is best to have a set way of reading palms. I start by examining the shape and texture of the hand, classifying the hand into a category (usually air, earth, fire, or water) in the process. I then take note of anything out of the ordinary, such as an exceptionally short Mercury finger. After this quick glance at the hand itself, I then look at the major lines in the following sequence: heart, head, life, and destiny. I then look at the thumb and the fingers, followed by the mounts. After this I look at the minor lines and the markings. With a quick reading I look only at the major hand and the process takes about five minutes. With a longer reading I am able to spend more time at every stage and examine both hands. My full-length readings take about an hour.

A Sample Reading

Here is an example of a brief palm reading for a man in his early forties (figure 49). I have included the palmistry reasons for the comments I make in parentheses. The first thing I noticed is that he is a good example of an air hand. His hands are firm and well cared for. They are pinkish in color.

You are a capable, practical, down-to-earth sort of person (shape of hand). *You can be placed into any sort of situation and will always rise upwards* (length of Jupiter finger).

Your heart line is strong and you have a combination of both pure types, the mental and physical. This is shown by the fork at the end of the line. It shows that you can see both sides of any situation. You are not nearly as romantic as you used to be. You can fall in love very easily, but your head always has something to say. Your love life has not always been smooth (indentations on the heart line), *but you come back up again immediately after any*

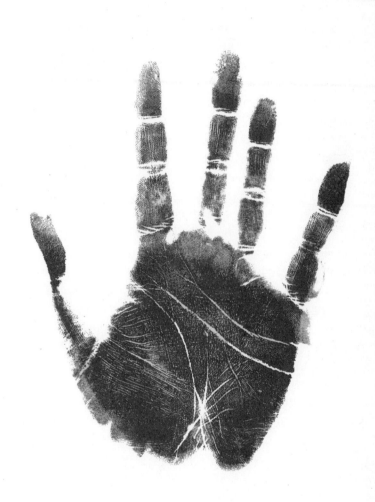

Figure 49: Print One

setback. You are a positive person and nothing can hold you down for long. It looks as if you are in a stable relationship that is continuing to grow and develop. You communicate well together, and this is one of the strongest aspects of your relationship (heart line, coupled with a glance at the first phalange of the Mercury finger).

Your head line is quite remarkable as it completely crosses your hand. This gives you a good brain, and makes you a detailed thinker (long head line, coupled with long fingers). *Anything you want to learn, you can learn thoroughly and quickly. In a sense you are learning all the way through your life. Your interests vary from time to time. It looks as if you become extremely serious about something and take it as far as you want, but then lose interest and move on to something else. Frequently, you try to do several things, all at the same time. There is a tendency to be impulsive. You frequently jump into things and then think about it afterwards* (space between head and life lines). *You are conscientious and responsible and you like to do things properly. You have the ability to grasp the essentials of a situation quickly and easily. You might become frustrated at people who take all day to make up their minds about something that you saw in a split second* (long head line, space between head and life lines, space between Apollo and Mercury fingers).

Your life line is clear and well marked. It comes well out across your palm, giving you plenty of stamina and energy. If you were doing something you enjoy, you could keep going almost indefinitely.

You take life pretty much as it comes. However, you worry when there is cause for it, as shown by these worry lines. The most serious ones are well behind you (worry lines crossing the life line in his middle to late twenties). *You have few worries compared to most people, and you are never worried for long.*

Your destiny line is interesting. It starts out as a strong line that is attached to your life line. This means that, despite your need for independence (space between head and life lines), *someone had a strong influence on you when you were very young. This was probably one or both of your parents.*

The fact that your destiny line began so strongly shows that you went into a career of some sort, and followed it through until about the age of twenty-seven or eight. At that point the destiny line changes. It gets both fainter and changes direction slightly. This means that the direction of your life also changed. You must have gone through a major reevaluation of your life at about that time. Your career probably changed, too, and for several years you were not 100 percent sure about where you were going, or what you wanted to do. About the age of thirty-four you found a new sense of direction and you are still following this new path.

You have a strong thumb. You are inclined to be stubborn when the situation demands it. You are easy to get along with but can certainly stand up for yourself when required (stiff thumb and strong mounts of Mars).

You have more logic than willpower (second phalange of the thumb longer than the first). *This means that you get great ideas, but do not always feel impelled to act upon them. Fortunately, you have enough drive and ambition in your hand to take advantage of your best ideas* (broad hand, strong destiny line, good head line, and long Jupiter finger).

You know how to get your own way (long Jupiter finger) *but you are tactful and diplomatic at the same time* (waisted second phalange of the thumb). *This is quite an art, and greatly enhances your people skills, which are excellent* (fingers held apart, good first phalange on the Mercury finger, and reasonable quadrangle).

You have a passionate nature (high, firm mount of Venus). *This usually relates to your love life, but also gives passion to everything you do. You are able to get excited and passionate about your dreams, goals, and interests.*

You have a strong little finger (when giving readings I do not use the palmistry terms for the fingers, since this confuses people). *It is set low, compared to the other fingers* (dropped little finger). *This means that everything goes well for a long while, but then you get dumped into something and have to climb out again. It often means learning the hard way. Everything takes longer than you would like* (the space between the head and life lines means he wants everything now) *and is harder than you would like* (dropped little finger).

You are an independent thinker and prefer to make your own mind up rather than taking too much on trust (wide space between the Apollo and Mercury fingers).

You have a good tip section on this finger. This shows that you have good communication skills, and would do well in any career that used your voice. You can also express yourself well with words on paper (long second phalange). *This is a talent that you could easily develop.*

The next finger (Apollo) *relates to creativity and beautiful things. You have natural good taste* (long middle phalange to the Apollo finger). *This means that you would be good at selling things that you personally found to be attractive* (middle phalange of the Apollo finger and tip phalange of the Mercury finger). *You are basically honest* (straight Mercury finger) *and would find it hard to sell anything that you did not like.*

The next finger (Saturn) *relates to limitations and restrictions. It also provides balance in our lives. We want that finger to be the longest in the hand, and we also want it to be as straight as possible. Your finger qualifies on both counts. This means that you have a sense of perspective about what is going on in your life, and you have good self-esteem.*

Your first finger (Jupiter) *is longer than your third* (Apollo) *finger. This gives you drive and energy. At times you may feel as if there is something inside you forcing you on to more and even greater accomplishments. This drive and energy is good, but you must remember to pause and relax and unwind every now and again. A long first finger is a mixed blessing. It gives you enthusiasm, energy, a healthy ego, ambition, and drive, all of which are wonderful qualities. However, some people with it drive themselves to an early grave since they don't know when to stop. You are fortunate in that you have learned to slow down and rest every now and again* (lack of stress, tension, and nervous energy lines).

The bottom section of this finger shows that you will develop an interest in philosophy or religion. This may or may not be a church type of religion. It could well be a philosophy of life that you build up and develop on your own. Whatever it is, it plays an increasingly important part in your life in the future.

You have a secure money sign (triangle created by destiny line, head line, and a minor line). *This gives you the potential to do extremely well financially* (the triangle is large). *However, it is crossed* (line bisecting the triangle). *That means that at times money will come easily, but at other times you may feel as if you are getting nowhere. Fortunately, you are persistent, and ultimately will do very well. You also come into money* (curving line under the Apollo finger). *Unfortunately, this line is not very helpful, since it does not say when you will come into this money, or how much is involved. However, at some stage in your life you will inherit money. There is no sign of any easy money, so you'll just have to earn it. Most of your money comes from hard work and good money management.*

You have a strong line of intuition coming down and touching your destiny line. You are an extremely logical person (long, straight head line and long fingers), *but you should also act on your feelings and hunches. You may, or may not, call this intuition, but you will find that these feelings always guide you in the right direction.*

You have several pronounced restlessness lines on your hand. These used to be called travel lines, and indicate that you are interested in new and different things, including travel. Judging from the strength of these lines I would say that you have traveled a great deal, and have quite a bit more travel in the future, as well.

You have one major line of romantic attachment (not visible on the palm print). *This shows that, although there may be any number of relationships, only one is of great importance in terms of your life. You are obviously inside that relationship right now* (relationship line comes up and over the side of the palm, and the quality of the heart line).

Your health appears to be excellent (broad hand, strong life line). *It looks as if you pay attention to physical fitness and look after yourself. This is your health line. It is basically strong and well marked. There was a time in your late twenties when the line became diffused for a while. That appears to have been an important time in your life, anyway, judging by the other lines. You probably would not want to repeat those years. However, the future looks good from a health point of view, and your life line remains clear and strong well into your old age.*

You are loyal to your friends and family. You are obviously a people person and would be happiest in a career where you were involved with others, preferably helping them in some way (humanitarian line running parallel to the destiny line inside the quadrangle; teacher's square below the Jupiter finger).

My guess, while reading this man's hand, was that he was either a teacher of some sort, or was dealing with items that he found to be attractive, possibly antiques. In fact, he had started out in life as a high school teacher, and had given that up in his late twenties to travel the world. He had found it hard to settle down again, which accounted for the disruption to most of the major lines in his late twenties. He is now a self-employed motivational speaker, and is perfectly suited for this field. His hand clearly reveals how suitable he is for this type of occupation:

He has a pronounced Jupiter finger, which gives a desire for leadership, and also indicates that he enjoys being the person who gives advice.

He has a good destiny line, which gives a sense of purpose and direction to his life.

He has a long Mercury finger, giving him excellent communication skills, both verbal and written. As a professional speaker he has to write his speeches. He has also written a book which he sells after his talks.

He is outgoing and enthusiastic, and has plenty of stamina and energy.

He has the potential to make a great deal of money, and usually this is best achieved through some form of self-employment.

He is independent. This is necessary as he spends several months of the year away from home presenting his talks in many different countries around the world.

This reading gives you some idea of the depth of information that can be provided in just a quick reading. Obviously, a full-length reading would provide a more comprehensive analysis, with much greater detail. I would also be able to be much more specific in my timing, since I could use dividers to accurately measure time. This man was right-handed, which is why I read this particular hand. His left hand would have been much more informative, since it would have told me what he is currently thinking about, which may be completely different to what he is actually doing.

A Second Reading

Here is another reading for a thirty-six year old woman (figure 50). Her main concern was relationships. She had been married twice, and had also been in another relationship that lasted for several years. She was now on her own and was wanting to know when the right man would enter her life. Consequently, this reading focuses mainly on this side of her life.

You are inclined to be emotional at times (water hand). *You are also inclined to worry, and this may even have affected your health in the past* (worry lines crossing the life line). *Fortunately, although you worry at times in the future, it is much more under control. This is a good sign. You have always felt things extremely deeply* (girdle of Venus). *This has not made life easy, particularly as far as relationships are concerned.*

You have had more ups and downs in this regard than most people (braiding along the heart line). *You have what is known as a mental heart line. This means that you need a partner who is caring, gentle, and tells you how much he loves you. You do not like vulgar, crude people, and the right person for you is likely to be refined and cultured.*

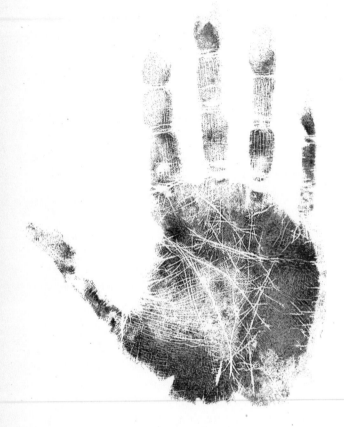

Figure 50: Print Two

You are inclined to be overly idealistic, at times (heart line is basically a mental one, but a fine line extends under the Jupiter finger). *This makes it hard for anyone to live up to your expectations. It also means that you probably find it hard to live up to your own expectations. Fortunately, your heart line gets easier, the further along it you go, so, speaking generally, your life is gradually getting smoother.*

You have a good brain and an excellent imagination (head line heads toward mount of Luna). *You use your brain well, but your emotions always win over logic, so they will always rule. There is nothing wrong with that, but your life would be easier if you slowed down and thought things through before acting.*

You have a strong life line, and you are fortunate in having a sister line that gives you added strength. It's like having two life lines, and you've needed that at times, particularly when these worry lines have crossed over your life line.

You have always been cautious, and it looks as if your upbringing, although close and loving, made it hard for you to become independent (head and life lines joined at commencement; destiny line starts inside the life line).

Your destiny line has changed direction a few times, reflecting the changes that have occurred in your life. You currently have a double destiny line, which means that you are doing at least two things at the same time. This is usually working as well as bringing up a family. The mere fact that you have a destiny line gives direction to your life, so you are going in the right direction, even though you probably do not realize that at the moment. In fact, your destiny line carries on well beyond your heart line and that means you will always be young at heart. You will never reach middle age inside.

You have a stubborn thumb, and I feel that you have used this to get your own way at times. You have simply dug your toes in and refused to budge (unyielding thumb, combined with a short Jupiter finger, giving lack of confidence and self-esteem). *This can be useful, but you need to ensure that you are stubborn only when absolutely necessary. Sometimes it pays to give in, just for the sake of peace and harmony. This is especially the case with close relationships.*

You have what is known as a "dropped" little finger. This means that everything goes well for a long while, and then, usually quite suddenly, everything goes wrong, and you have to work hard to extricate yourself. You could say that it means learning the hard way.

You have good communication skills, particularly in writing (long second phalange on the Mercury finger). *Sometimes it might be easier to put your thoughts and feelings down on paper, rather than say them out loud. You could well have a talent for writing poetry* (hand is basically an emotional one).

You appreciate nice things around you and work best in a pleasant environment (second phalange of Apollo finger). *You could also make money out of things that you found to be attractive. In your case, this could well be some form of writing.*

You have a strong, straight middle finger, but your first finger is shorter than your ring finger. This means that you lacked confidence early on in life. This may have held you back at that time, but this finger is now a blessing, since it means that you know when to stop. You will not kill yourself by overdoing things. You pause to rest and relax along the way. However, getting started may sometimes be the hardest part of the whole exercise (logic section of the thumb longer than the willpower).

You have a ring of Solomon running around your first finger. This gives an interest in the psychic world. You also have a strong line of intuition, so you could develop that a long way, if you wanted to. I feel that you already make good use of this talent. For instance, you can probably sum people up the instant you meet them, and your first impressions are almost always correct.

You have a nice, clear money sign. This is over a lifetime, and does not necessarily reflect your current situation. Certainly, you will end up comfortably off, and will have no major money worries in your old age.

You have several, clearly marked restlessness lines on your hand. These used to be known as travel lines, and it looks as if there have been a number of times in your life when you would have liked to simply let go of everything and travel away to some exotic location. You've done that in your mind, but there is also actual travel shown, as well. It looks as if you make the most of each trip you do (six extremely long and clear restlessness lines), *but you like coming home again as well.*

Your health line is clear and well marked. You are fortunate in having a strong constitution. Although worry has definitely affected your health in the past, it will play a smaller role in the future. You appear to pay more attention to physical fitness in the future, and this also, of course, plays a part in promoting good health.

In many ways, you are at a turning point in your life. The worst worry of your life is now a year or so behind you (worry line crossing life line at age thirty-five). You are on an even keel again (clear destiny line) and emotionally life is becoming much smoother (she is now immediately beyond the worst island on her heart line). I don't think you are quite ready for a new relationship yet, but that person is not far away. It looks to me as if it will take a while for the relationship to fully develop. You will be extremely cautious, which is not surprising when you look at the past in your heart line. However, it will be worth the wait. I can see much happiness in your future.

Again, this gives you some idea about the amount of information that can be given in just a quick reading.

Practice giving brief readings whenever you can. You will find that most people will be delighted to show you their hands. You will learn something from every hand you look at, and you will have a never-ending opportunity to make people feel good about themselves and their lives.

12

Making Palm Prints

It is a comparatively simple matter to take palm prints of people's hands. They are useful in a number of ways:

You can see how someone's hands change over a period of time. I took prints of my children's hands as they were growing up, and it is fascinating to see their different interests reflected in their hands at an extremely early age. It was interesting to see how their hands changed as they grew, and as their interests changed.

You can see health factors much more clearly on a palm print than you can on the hands.

You can measure time more accurately on a print than you can from the hand itself.

You will gradually build up a collection of different prints that you can examine whenever you wish.

You can do original research. You may find an unusual marking on someone's hand and not know what it means. You can check your collection of prints to see if anyone else you have read for has the same formation. This is an excellent way to learn, and you may be able to add something valuable to the art.

Nowadays, I frequently take photocopies of people's hands. These are excellent for examining the lines, skin ridge patterns, and other markings, but are not perfect, since the shape of the hand is distorted in the process. I still find it preferable to take palm prints whenever possible.

To do this you will need to obtain an ink roller and a tube of water-based black ink. I prefer black ink to blue, and use a water-based ink because it cleans off easily. I have occasionally used lipstick to make palm prints when I have been away from home and nothing else was available.

Fingerprint ink makes the best prints, but it is oil based and is much harder to clean off the hands. I used to use fingerprint ink all the time. I now use it only when I am taking palm prints of someone famous, or am reading for someone with some particularly unusual features on their hands.

You will find a selection of rollers and inks at any store that sells supplies for artists. I like a roller that is four inches wide. This is because smaller rollers often leave edge marks on the print.

You will also need some good quality bond paper and a slightly spongy surface to make the print on. I used to use the rubber pad that old-fashioned typewriters rested on, but many years ago changed to a one-inch stack of tea towels.

The paper is placed on top of the tea towels in readiness. Squeeze a small amount of ink on to a pane of glass or a spare piece of bond paper. Roll it with the roller until it is smooth, and the roller is covered with an even coating of ink.

Ask the person to remove any rings they may be wear-
ing, and then hold their hands out in front of you. Starting
from the wrist end, cover the palms with a fine coating of
ink. This is best done using long, even strokes of the roller.
Naturally, some people have a deep area in the middle of
the palm and you may have to use small, fine movements
to ensure that the entire palm is evenly covered.

Ask the person to hold their hands naturally and to press
both hands simultaneously onto the sheet of paper that is
waiting on the tea towels. Once they have done this, press
down gently on the backs of their hands to ensure that the
middle of the palm makes an impression on the paper.

Hold down each end of the paper and ask your client to
lift both hands straight upwards. This reveals the print and
you can quickly examine it to see if it is good enough.

If the center of the palm has not left an impression, you
will have to do it again. This time, though, after they have
placed their hands on the sheet of paper, have them raise
their hands in the air with the paper still attached. You can
then gently press the paper into the hollow of their palms,
before peeling the paper away.

I always take a separate print of the thumbs. This is
because only the side of the thumb is printed in a palm
print, and it is valuable to have a record of the thumb itself.

I discovered early on that it is a good idea to take your
client to the bathroom after making the prints, and to turn
the taps on for him or her. This saves a tremendous amount
of cleaning up later.

Usually, my clients like to take their palm prints away
with them. Because of this, I ask if I can make a second

print so that I have one for my files. Occasionally, someone will refuse, but most of the time people are flattered that I want to keep a copy of their prints in my collection.

I identify and date the prints. I also make any necessary notes about the person's hands on another piece of paper. For instance, one of the mounts may be extremely high, but this may not be apparent on the palm print. It is useful to keep information like this for future reference.

Some palmists have a separate data sheet that they fill in on every pair of hands they look at. They may, for instance, make notes about the temperature of the hand, the amount of hair on the back of the hand, the softness or firmness of the hand, et cetera. I did do this at one time, but now simply make notes of the items that I consider to be important for each particular person.

I file the prints alphabetically. Some palmists use other systems of filing based on different features of the hand. This can be useful for research purposes, but can make it hard to quickly locate a particular set of prints at a later date. By filing the prints alphabetically, I can easily find my clients' prints when they return for another reading. I find it endlessly fascinating to see how people's hands change from one visit to the next. Sometimes, dramatic changes can occur in just a few months.

It takes practice to become good at taking palm prints. Once you become used to it, you will find that you obtain perfect prints almost every time. It is easier to take prints of one hand at a time, and you may prefer to do it this way. I prefer to do both hands at once, on the same sheet of paper.

13

Conclusion

You now have all the basics of palmistry at your disposal. Naturally, it will take a while to absorb everything. The best way to learn is to look at as many hands as you can. Compare the hands of married couples. See if you can examine the hands of three or four generations from the same family. Compare the hands of a group of friends, looking for both similarities and differences. Do not be afraid to ask questions.

Read as much as you can on the subject. I have more than four hundred books on palmistry in my personal library, and still buy almost every new book that appears on this subject. I have been involved with this subject for more than forty years, but am still learning. Naturally, I do not agree with everything that I read, but different viewpoints force me to re-examine things and possibly see them in a different light.

You will find that most people will be thrilled to show you their hands. Palmistry is a wonderful way to make new friends. It will help you to understand other people's motivations, as well as your own. You will be able to help many people with your new skill.

I hope that palmistry will fascinate you for as long as you live.

Notes

Introduction

1. In fact, every reference to palmistry in the Bible is favorable: "[H]e said, 'Wherefore doth my lord thus pursue after his servant? for what have I done? or what evil is in my hand?'" (1 Sam. 26:18); "Length of days is in her right hand; and in her left hand riches and honor" (Prov. 3:16); "Behold I have graven thee on the palms of my hands; thy walls are continually before me" (Isa. 49:16).

2. Adolphe A. Desbarrolles, *Révélations complètes* (Paris: Vigot frères, 1859. Reprinted 1922).

3. Casimir Stanislaus d'Arpentigny, *La chirognomie, ou l'art de reconnaître les tendances de l'intelligence d'après les formes de la main* (Paris: Charles le Clere, 1843). My friends gave me a copy of the first English translation of this book one year for Christmas. The English title is *The Science of the Hand*, translated by Ed. Heron-Allen (London: Ward, Lock and Bowden, 1865).

Chapter One

1. George Muchary, *Traite complet de la chiromancie deductive et experimental* (Paris: Editions du Chariot, 1958).

Chapter Two

1. Richard Webster, *Revealing Hands* (St. Paul: Llewellyn Publications, 1994), p. 87.

Chapter Three

1. William G. Benham, *The Laws of Scientific Hand Reading* (New York: Duell, Sloan and Pearce, 1900), p. 380.

2. Adolphe Desbarrolles, *Les Mystères de la main* (Paris: Garnier frères, 1859).

3. Desbarrolles, *Révélations complètes*.

4. Henri Mangin, *La Main, miroir du destin* (Paris: Editions Fernand Sorlot, 1939).

Chapter Four

1. Comte C. de Saint-Germain, *The Practice of Palmistry for Professional Purposes*. This book was originally published in 1897, and is still available in many editions. I consider it to be one of the worst books on the subject of palmistry.

Chapter Six

1. Benham, *The Laws of Scientific Handreading*; William Benham, *How to Choose Vocations from the Hand* (reprinted by Sagar Publications, New Delhi, 1974).

Chapter Nine

1. James S. Thompson and Margaret W. Thompson, *Genetics in Medicine* (Philadelphia: W. B. Saunders Company, 1966), p. 244.

2. Harold Cummins, M.D., and Charles Midlo, *Finger-prints, Palms and Soles* (New York: Dover Publications, 1943).

3. Beryl Hutchinson, *Your Life in Your Hands* (London: Neville Spearman Limited, 1967), p. 110.

Chapter Ten

1. There are many serious medical books that discuss dermatoglyphics (the study of skin ridge patterns). One of the most approachable of these is *Dermatoglyphics in Medical Disorders* by Blanka Schaumann and Milton Alter (New York: Springer-Verlag, 1976). A book on medical palmistry written for the general public is *Medical Palmistry: Health and Character in the Hand* by Marten Steinback (Secaucus, NJ: University Books, 1975).

2. Charles Dickens, *David Copperfield* (first published in 1850; numerous editions available).

Glossary

Arch. The arch is one of the three main types of finger-print patterns.

Destiny Line. A line that runs from the base of the palm toward the fingers. It provides a sense of direction to a person's life.

Girdle of Venus. The girdle of Venus is a line, or series of lines, that runs parallel to the heart line, between the heart line and the fingers. People with this line are extremely sensitive.

Head Line. A line that runs across the palm, starting close to or joined to the life line. The quality of this line reveals the person's intellect and manner of thinking.

Heart Line. The heart line is the major line that runs across the palm, close to the fingers. It reveals the person's emotional life.

Knotty Fingers. This is the term used to describe fingers with prominent knuckles.

Life Line. The life line encircles the thumb, and reveals the person's energy and vitality.

Loop. A loop is a skin ridge pattern, oval or round in shape, that is found on the palm of the hand.

Mounts. There are nine mounts found on the hand, named after the planets. They are usually raised areas on the surface of the palm. The quality and quantity of these reveal the person's interests.

Percussion. The percussion is the term used to describe the edge of the palm running from the little finger to the wrist.

Phalange. A phalange is one section of a finger or thumb.

Rascettes. The rascettes are the lines that cross the wrist at the base of the hand. There are usually three of them. In the past, Gypsies said that each one represented twenty-five years of life.

Simian Crease. The simian crease (sometimes known as the simian line) occurs when the head and heart line become a single line that runs across the palm.

Smooth Fingers. Smooth fingers do not have prominent joints, and appear smooth throughout their length.

Tri-Radius. A tri-radius is a small triangular shape that is formed by the skin ridge patterns. It frequently looks like a three-pointed star.

Whorl. The whorl is a skin ridge pattern that looks like a series of concentric circles. It is one of the three main types of fingerprint patterns, and is also found in loops on the surface of the palm.

Suggested Reading

Altman, Nathaniel. *The Palmistry Workbook*. Northamptonshire, UK: Aquarian Press, 1984.

Altman, Nathaniel and Andrew Fitzherbert. *Career, Success, and Self-Fulfillment*. Northamptonshire, UK: Aquarian Press, 1988.

Aria, Gopi. *Palmistry for the New Age*. Long Beach, CA: Morningland, 1977.

Asano, Hachiro. *Hands: The Complete Book of Palmistry*. Tokyo: Japan Publications, 1985.

Bashir, Mir. *How to Read Hands*. London: Thorsons Publishers, 1955.

———. *The Art of Hand Analysis*. London: Frederick Muller, 1973.

Benham, William G. *The Laws of Scientific Handreading*. New York: Duell, Sloan & Pearce, 1900. Republished as *The Benham Book of Palmistry*. Van Nuys, CA: Newcastle Publishing, 1988.

———. *How to Choose Vocations from the Hand*. New York: Knickerbocker Press, 1901.

Brandon-Jones, David. *Practical Palmistry*. London: Rider & Co., 1981.

Brandon-Jones, David and Veronica Bennett. *Your Palm: Barometer of Health*. London: Rider & Co., 1985.

———. *The Palmistry of Love*. London: Arrow Books, 1980.

———. *Your Hand and Your Career*. London: Arrow Books, 1980.

Brenner, Elizabeth. *The Hand Book*. Millbrae, CA: Celestial Arts, 1980.

———. *Hand in Hand*. Millbrae, CA: Celestial Arts, 1981.

Chawdhri, L. R. *A Handbook of Palmistry*. New Delhi, India: Hind Pocket Books, 1980.

Cummins, Harold and Charles Midlo. *Fingerprints, Palms and Soles*. New York: Dover Publications, 1943.

Domin, Linda. *Palmascope: The Instant Palm Reader*. St. Paul, MN: Llewellyn Publications, 1993.

Dukes, Shifu Terence. *Chinese Hand Analysis*. York Beach, ME: Samuel Weiser, 1987.

Fenton-Smith, Paul. *Palmistry Revealed*. East Roseville, Australia: Simon & Schuster Australia, 1996.

Fitzherbert, Andrew. *Hand Psychology*. London: Angus & Robertson, 1986.

Galton, Francis. *Fingerprints*. New York: Da Capo Press, 1965.

Gettings, Fred. *The Book of the Hand*. London: Paul Hamlyn, 1965.

———. *The Book of Palmistry*. London: Triune Press, 1974.

———. *Palmistry Made Easy*. London: Bancroft & Co., 1966.

Hipskind, Judith. *The New Palmistry*. St. Paul, MN: Llewellyn Publications, 1994.

———. *Palmistry: The Whole View*. St. Paul, MN: Llewellyn Publications, 1977.

Hutchinson, Beryl. *Your Life in Your Hands*. London: Neville Spearman, 1967.

Jaegers, Beverly C. *You and Your Hand*. Cottonwood, AZ: Esoteric Publications, 1974.

Lawrance, Myrah. *Hand Analysis*. West Nyack, NJ: Parker Publishing, 1967.

Luxon, Bettina and Jill Goolden. *Your Hand: Simple Palmistry for Everyone*. London: William Heinemann, 1983.

Masters, Anthony. *Mind Map*. London: Eyre Methuen, 1980.

Nakagaichi, Mila. *Palmistry for the Global Village*. Tokyo: Tachibana Shuppan, 1998.

Newcomer-Bramblett, Esther. *Reading Hands for Pleasure or Profit*. Austin, TX: Woods Publications, 1982.

Nishitani, Yasuto. *Palmistry Revolution*. Tokyo: Tachibana Shuppan, 1992.

Sherson, R. *The Key to Your Hands*. Auckland, New Zealand: Mystical Books, 1973.

Squire, Elizabeth Daniels. *Palmistry Made Practical*. New York: Fleet Press, 1960.

Webster, Richard. *Revealing Hands*. St. Paul, MN: Llewellyn Publications, 1994.

West, Peter. *Life Lines: An Introduction to Palmistry*. Northamptonshire, UK: Aquarian Press, 1981.

Wilson, Joyce. *The Complete Book of Palmistry*. New York: Bantam Books, 1971.

Out-of-print books that are well worth tracking down:

d'Arpentigny, Casimer Stanislas. *The Science of the Hand.* Translated by Ed. Heron Allen. London: Ward, Lock & Bowden, 1865.

Frith, Henry. *Palmistry Secrets Revealed.* London: Ward Lock & Co., 1952.

———. *Practical Palmistry.* London: Ward Lock & Co., n.d.

Jaquin, Noel. *The Hand Speaks.* London: Lyndoe & Fisher, 1941.

———. *The Human Hand: The Living Symbol.* London: Rockliff Publishing, 1956.

———. *Scientific Palmistry.* London: Faber & Faber, n.d. Reprint, New Delhi: Sagar, 1967.

———. *The Hand of Man.* London: Faber & Faber, 1933.

———. *Hand-Reading Made Easy.* London: C. Arthur Pearson, 1928.

———. *The Signature of Time.* London: Faber & Faber, 1950.

St. Hill, Katherine. *The Book of the Hand.* London: Rider & Co., 1927.

———. *Grammar of Palmistry.* London: Sampson, Low, Marston & Co., 1893.

Spier, Julius. *The Hands of Children.* London: Routledge & Kegan Paul, 1955. Reprint, New Delhi: Sagar, 1973.

Wolff, Charlotte. *The Human Hand.* London: Methuen & Co., 1943.

———. *The Hand in Psychological Diagnosis.* London: Methuen & Co., 1971. Reprint, New Delhi: Sagar, 1972.

Index

Numerology for Beginners
Easy Guide to Love • Money • Destiny

GERIE BAUER

Every letter and number in civilization has a particular power, or vibration. For centuries, people have read these vibrations through the practice of numerology. References in the Bible even describe Jesus using numerology to change the names of his disciples. *Numerology for Beginners* is a quick ready-to-use reference that lets you find your personal vibrations based on the numbers associated with your birth date and name.

Within minutes, you will be able to assess the vibrations surrounding a specific year, month, and day—even a specific person. Detect whether you're in a business cycle or a social cycle, and whether a certain someone or occupation would be compatible with you. Plus, learn to detect someone's personality within seconds of learning their first name!

1-56718-057-4
5 ³/₁₆ x 8, 336 pp. $9.95

To order, call 1-800-THE MOON
Prices subject to change without notice

Aura Reading for Beginners
Develop Your Psychic Awareness for Health & Success

RICHARD WEBSTER

When you lose your temper, don't be surprised if a dirty red haze suddenly appears around you. If you do something magnanimous, your aura will expand. Now you can learn to see the energy that emanates off yourself and other people through the proven methods taught by Richard Webster in his psychic training classes.

Learn to feel the aura, see the colors in it, and interpret what those colors mean. Explore the chakra system, and how to restore balance to chakras that are over- or understimulated. Then you can begin to imprint your desires into your aura to attract what you want in your life.

1-56718-798-6
5 3/16 x 8, 208 pp., illus. $9.95

To order, call 1-800-THE MOON
Prices subject to change without notice

Palmistry

The Whole View

Judith Hipskind

Here is a unique approach to palmistry! Judy Hipskind not only explains how to analyze hands, but also explains why hand analysis works. The approach is based on a practical rationale and is easy to understand. Over 130 illustrations accompany the informal, positive view of hand analysis.

This new approach to palmistry avoids categorical predictions and presents the meaning of the palm as a synthesis of many factors: the shape, gestures, flexibility, mounts, and lives of each hand—as well as a combination of the effects of both heredity and the environment. No part of the hand is treated as a separate unit; the hand reflects the entire personality. An analysis based on the method presented in this book is a rewarding experience for the client—a truly whole view!

0-87542-306-X

5 1/4 x 8, 248 pp., illus. $9.95